"Let's say that Rick is my friend and he is in pain. Because he is my friend, that causes me pain, but I don't like to feel his pain. So what I'd like to do is to heal Rick as quickly as I possibly can to get rid of my pain. I'd like to give him some kind of easy answer, like: 'Oh, I'm sorry your mother died but don't feel bad about it. She's gone to heaven.' Or: 'I had that problem once, and all you have to do is go running.'"

"But more often than not the most healing thing that we can do with someone who is in pain, rather than trying to get rid of that pain, is to sit there and be willing to share it. We have to learn to hear and to bear other people's pain" (M. Scott Peck, *Further Along the Road Less Traveled*, pp. 27, 28).

# WHEN GOD'S HEART
# BREAKS

# Richard W. Coffen

REVIEW AND HERALD® PUBLISHING ASSOCIATION
HAGERSTOWN, MD 21740

Unless otherwise noted, all Bible verses cited are from the *Holy Bible,
New International Version*. Copyright © 1973, 1978, 1984, International
Bible Society. Used by permission of Zondervan Bible Publishers.

Texts credited to Anchor are from Judges *(Anchor Bible)*, translated and
edited by Robert G. Baling. Copyright © 1975 by Doubleday & Company,
Inc.

Bible texts credited to CEV are from the Contemporary English Version.
Copyright © American Bible Society, 1991, 1995. Used by permission.

Bible texts credited to Jerusalem are from *The Jerusalem Bible*, copyright
© 1966 by Darton, Longman & Todd, Ltd., and Doubleday & Company,
Inc. Used by permission of the publisher.

Bible texts credited to NRSV are from the New Revised Standard
Version of the Bible, copyright © 1989 by the Division of Christian
Education of the National Council of the Churches of Christ in the U.S.A.
Used by permission.

This book was
Edited by Gerald Wheeler
Designed by Dale Chapman
Typeset: 11/13 Galliard


PRINTED IN U.S.A.

01 00 99 98 97          5 4 3 2 1


**R&H Cataloging Service**
Coffen, Richard Wayne, 1941-
       When God's heart breaks.

       1. Suffering—Religious aspects—Christianity.
I. Title.

               231.8



ISBN 0-8280-1070-6

# DEDICATION

Dedicated to
Rosalia, who loves me
always and anyway,
and
Bob and Ron, who
invariably make my day.

# CONTENTS

# A FEW PRELIMINARY WORDS

---

D r. Jere Patzer had invited me as a guest on his monthly radio program *Issues and Interviews*. He wanted to discuss my book *When God Sheds Tears*, which deals with some of the same issues addressed in the book you now hold in your hands—the problem of disaster, disease, and death and how we respond to such evils.

"How is it that you wrote a book on the topic of suffering?" he asked.

Since I had anticipated that he might pose such a question, I had mulled over in my mind how I might respond, but I'm afraid that my nervousness at being interviewed on live radio did not make for a very lucid explanation. So now in the quiet of my Byte Room (the comfortable place at home where my wife and I keep our computer equipment), I'll try to set down what perhaps will be a bit more coherent answer.

Basically three events—or clusters of events—have piqued my interest in the topic and brought me to this point of writing yet a second book as something of a supplement to *When God Sheds Tears*.

The first cluster of events has to do with my extended family, which has been plagued with a great deal of personal distress.

My mother cannot recall a single day when she hasn't had a headache. It's just that sometimes the headaches turn into migraines, which lay her low. So commonplace are even severe headaches that Mother generally resorts to fibbing when asked how she is. A chronic answer such as "Oh, my head's splitting!" would wear thin pretty quickly.

My father broke the same ankle twice. The first time, his entire leg showed early stages of blood poisoning, even though the orthopedic physician insisted that all looked normal to him, including the red streaks shooting up Dad's leg like lightning bolts. This led to an early retirement, followed by a massive heart attack. Since then every time the phone rang, my heart jumped inside, because it just might be Mother with the worst of news. Indeed, on December 17, 1994, around 3:30 in the morning the ringing phone awakened us. It was Mother, phoning from California. Dad had just died—suddenly and unexpectedly—after having put in a full day of activity. Quickly I made flight reservations and was in California just hours later. So much for a merry Christmas season in 1994!

My twin uncles, John and Jim, have likewise suffered through a lifetime of incapacitating migraines. Aunt Dolly, Uncle John's wife, has been diagnosed as having Parkinson's. And for some 30 years Aunt Eleanor suffered from multiple sclerosis. Her sister, my aunt Vera, was crippled with rheumatoid arthritis for pretty much all her adult life. When I saw her daughter Gayle at Aunt Eleanor's funeral, she looked like a faxed copy of her deceased mother—shuffling movements and grotesquely swollen knuckles. And Gayle's daughter LoAnne continues the macabre tradition. Alzheimer's disease has destroyed the mind of beautiful Aunt Frances. Uncle Malcolm apparently has Huntington's disease. Around the time of my birth, Aunt Ruth (yet another of Mother's sisters) bled to death from a coat hanger abortion performed by her attorney lover. Cousin Denny was little more than a skeleton when he succumbed to cystic fibrosis as a teenager. And gaunt, haggard Butchie, another cousin, died of the same.

The second event occurred during 1962 in homiletics class at college. My text was Jeremiah 44:16-18, 23, and I had titled my sermon "The Barometer of God's Love." True to the demands of the homiletical discipline, I had a proposition (the sermon in a single sentence): "God's love is not measured by abundance or want, but by Calvary." Twelve fellow students, in addition to my major professor, constituted the congregation of guinea pigs. Each had in hand an 8½"x 11" "Sermon Analysis" form and was to score such factors as delivery, physical appearance, content, theology, and spirit. Each of the major headings subdivided into other aspects: volume, inflection, articulation, dress, facial features, posture, coherence, emphasis, unity, clarity, beauty, force, accuracy, vividness, biblical background, summary, length, dignity, persuasiveness, and sincerity, among others.

I still have those evaluation forms in my file. Each student was especially kind. Darrel, clearly the most eloquent speaker in our class, gave me 31 fives (highest scores) and six fours. (Because he came to class late, he did not score me on the four other elements on the list.) Herm also was generous and wrote, "I really enjoyed your sermon. Good logic here!" Dick reported, "Had some wonderful insights."

Luis, a Hispanic student, was overly kind. He scored me with "superiors" except for four "very goods." "You did answer many questions that I had about suffering. I like very much your own thinking and observations." Chris, a German student whom I respected, encouraged me with these words: "I like your practical thinking on God's love."

As always, the comments of Herbert Douglass, my major professor, helped me most—both the negative and positive. His high marks meant much more to me, of course, than those given by my fellow students. But one of his comments was especially rewarding: "Your logic is inescapable."

Those four words encouraged me more than anything else written on those evaluation sheets, though many of the students' comments reinforced Douglass's observation. Suddenly I felt more at home with the power that results by combining scriptural insight with careful logic. Clearly reason and revelation together can complement each other. They are not opposites that we must choose between. And both can be—and must be—applied with rigor to the problem of suffering.

That positive reinforcement back in 1962 has stayed with me through the ensuing years and has empowered me to continue addressing our reactions to the absurdity of evil in the world.

The final event likewise came with much poignancy.

During the 1980s 4-year-old Melody drowned in a small pond in a neighbor's yard (see *When God Sheds Tears,* pp. 31, 32). At the funeral the pastor encouraged the grieving parents to acquiesce to God's will.

Several friends attending the service said later they had been praying that God would give the parents the gift of deaf ears so that they would not hear (or at least not understand) what the well-meaning preacher was saying. Surely his suggestion was the height of heresy at worst and insensitivity at best!

And, of course, other tragedies befalling friends and ac- quaintances and learning what intentioned well-wishers had said and done in response (appropriately and inappropriately) have likewise had an impact on my thinking.

These clusters of events have profoundly affected me, moti- vating me to redouble my efforts in addressing the disaster, dis- ease, and death that stalk our lives. With each day that passes, the enigma grows more potent and trenchant. What do you tell yourself? And what do you declare to those who are agonizing and grieving? Or *not* say?

But before you plunge into reading the remainder of *When God's Heart Breaks,* you should be aware of the highly important things enumerated below.

First, this book is *not* a theodicy. "Theodicy" is a theological word that comes from two Greek words: *theos,* which means God; and *dikē,* which can indicate something such as "judged" or "justified." (You are undoubtedly aware of the word "Laodicea," which appears in the last book of the Bible. It was a city in Asia Minor, and scholars usually explain it as consisting of two Greek words: *laos,* meaning people; and *dikē.* The typical interpretation of the word is that it means "the people are judged," though it might also be construed as "the people are justified.")

A theodicy, then, is a reasoned approach in which we judge God (more typically defend or justify) to be fair despite the prevalence of suffering, especially what appears to be gratuitous suffering, in the world. Theodicy is a highly philosophical enterprise and requires extreme precision in thought and word.

Many theodicies have been written, some of them more helpful than others and some more easily understood than others. Ronald H. Nash is professor of philosophy at Western Kentucky University. As a trained philosopher with an evangelical worldview, Nash has written a helpful theodicy titled *Faith and Reason—Searching for a Rational Faith*. Among the topics broached is the problem of evil and the suffering that comes in its train. "Every philosopher I know believes that the most serious challenge to theism [belief in God] was, is, and will continue to be the problem of evil" (p. 177). Only the naive, I suspect, would disagree with him.

Nash goes on to point out something very interesting. In defending the doctrine of God in the face of disaster, disease, and death, the argumentation the believer presents must be logical. "When a theist offers a defense (as opposed to a theodicy), all he is attempting to do is show that his belief in God is plausible, rational, or consistent in the face of difficulties raised by the presence of evil" (p. 188). The defense attempts to "prove" nothing but does try "to show the coherence of theism by offering *logically possible reasons* why God permits evil" (*ibid.;* italics supplied).

As a result, the propositions in the syllogisms that Christians use in rationalizing the existence of both God and evil need to be "logically consistent" and "logically possible." But they do not need to be "true"—only "possibly true. And . . . it is not necessary that anyone actually believe . . . or even think that [the proposition] is possible. What is necessary is that [the proposition] describe a logically possible state of affairs . . . whether in fact it is or is not true" (*ibid.*, p. 187).

Nash continues his discussion by providing helpful insights. His rigorous philosophical training and Christian ardor fill the entire book, making it insightful reading. As F. F. Bruce observed about Nash's argumentation: "Nash is not content with refuting unsound arguments; he makes positive contributions to the subject under discussion" (from the dust jacket).

Nash's presentation appears to follow stringent logical rules. He feels that it is entirely possible to argue logically, cogently, and effectively that the existence of a good God is *not* inherently incompatible with the presence of disaster, disease, and death. And his rigidly disciplined writing is truly helpful.

But on page 198 Nash adds an interesting footnote that almost undoes everything he had earlier argued for: "While the answers offered . . . may be valuable as far as they go, the really difficult questions arise when one is trying to find a reason for some *specific instance of evil* such as the slow, painful death of a child. It is one thing to claim to understand why natural or moral evil in general exists; it is something else to try to understand why some specific instance of moral or natural evil exists. . . . When we turn to specific instances of evil, I think the wise theist will admit his ignorance."

Good advice, don't you think? And that's where this book and my previous book, *When God Sheds Tears,* come in. I'm not skilled enough to write a carefully reasoned defense of why the suffering that mars our world is quite congruous with the existence of an all-wise, all-powerful, all-loving God (as Nash did). Although I enjoy reading such philosophical approaches, my own mind isn't sufficiently sharp to follow all the lines of argumentation or to set them out in a better or more understandable format myself.

Truth is, I don't have all the answers. In fact, I have precious few answers. Well, let me be completely honest: *When it comes to children being tortured and adults suffering incomprehensible pain, it all seems terribly absurd—at least to me.*

So as you read this book, don't expect me to defend God in the face of the atrocities that curse our planet. I'm simply not up to it. As I said, this book is not a theodicy and therefore has a much more modest purpose. More about that a little later.

Second, a cherished friend and colleague has gently chided me more than once about this book. "The stories you tell here are extreme, even radical, cases. They don't reflect the run-of-the-mill suffering that most of us encounter."

He's absolutely right! I have chosen to relate these true stories of radically drastic pain and suffering for two reasons.

1. Because of their very nature, these stories are highly dra-

matic. They reach out, smash through your chest, and grab you by the heart. *When God's Heart Breaks* has plenty of competition. Numerous things beckon for your attention—dirty dishes, *Home Improvement,* a growing lawn, clothes in need of ironing, *Discover* magazine, and a hundred other enticements. So I looked for striking stories bursting with poignancy—something assured of grabbing your attention.

2. The everyday troubles that bother us typically don't have the power to trigger the kinds of questions in our minds that sensational incidents of suffering do. For many of us (maybe most of us) the things we "suffer" tend to be more nuisances than anything else.

When a woman who jumped a stoplight and tried to turn left from the right-hand lane broadsided my van, I was really annoyed. She came charging out of her car and scolded me for appearing out of nowhere (no, I did not suddenly materialize despite her accusation) and speeding through a traffic light (which I had been stopped at for about a minute). Why in the world did it have to happen to me? Why was I at that intersection at that precise instant? Why not someone else? But the incident was really more annoying than serious. Insurance covered the cost of repairing and repainting the van. I was still able to drive it to work until the time for the repairs. (She had to have her car towed away.) And the accident did not cause me to call into question God's justice or mercy.

Then there was the time I awoke in the middle of the night with a pain that quickly burgeoned from a nuisance to something requiring medical attention—stat! The kidney stone hurt so much that it took sheer grit to keep from passing out while I was supposed to fill out the requisite forms at the emergency room. But even that acute pain didn't trigger my philosophical side. I didn't lie there ruminating about how a good God could let bad things happen to such a good person as I.

Permit me one more personal example. Since 1963 my immune system has been attacking my gastrointestinal tract. As a result, in past years I have hemorrhaged so severely that I've spent a Christmas in the hospital. And one summer, because of a lack of blood, I fainted while delivering a sermon at church! If the odds of your winning the powerball lottery were as high as my chances of developing colon cancer as a result of this disease, you'd probably be wise to play!

Yet once again I do not find myself wrestling with the big issues involved in trying to relate a good God to the bad things that happen. My condition doesn't force me into introspection about the unfairness of life. After all, each of us copes with one difficulty or another. That's simply par for the course here on our planet.

But I felt much different when I heard about 3-year-old Caitlin. On June 18, 1993, the tent she was sleeping in caught on fire from a citronella candle, and as a result 90 percent of her little body was burned—50 percent of that was *fourth*-degree burns.

Now, I looked through about a half dozen sources to learn about fourth-degree burns. None of them mentioned them. Most medical dictionaries and encyclopedia entries about burns mention only first-, second-, and third-degree burns.

But there *is* such a thing as a fourth-degree burn. It is a deep burn that goes through the skin and into the underlying tissue—even into the muscle, connective tissues, and the bone itself. According to *Encyclopaedia Britannica:* "Fourth-degree burns are of grave prognosis, particularly if they involve more than a small portion of the body" (vol. 15, p. 378).

It was *not* a small part of Caitlin's body that was burned. Much of it was charred. *Encyclopaedia Britannica* goes on to state that the mortality rate for burns can be worked out by a simple formula. Take the percentage of the body that was burned, add the victim's age in years, and that equals the mortality rate. In Caitlin's case, then, you'd take 90 and add 3, getting a 93 percent mortality rate.

When I heard about this tragedy, my mind went into high gear. All sorts of questions flooded my thinking processes. Here was a situation of such magnitude that one could only wonder about the fairness of life and the goodness of God. All the finely spun theodicies I had read seemed little more than a mockery in the face of this practically unthinkable turn of events.

Since this tragic accident occurred during a religious revival retreat, the next day many prayed for a miracle.

Ah yes! Didn't we all want a miracle for Caitlin! But why expect a miracle *now*?

Why hadn't there been a *teeny-weeny, itsy-bitsy miracle* the night before, snuffing out the flickering flame on the citronella candle? One strong breeze blowing through the tent could have taken care of that.

Or why hadn't God performed a *pint-sized miracle* that would have kept the molten wax from igniting?

Or why not a *regular-sized miracle* that would have prevented the tent canvas, which was flame-retardant in the first place, from catching fire?

But there had been *no teeny-weeny, itsy-bitsy miracle* when Caitlin had been tucked into bed.

There had been *no pint-sized miracle* at 10:00 p.m.

And there had been *no regular-sized miracle* at 11:30.

So why on earth should anyone expect a *giant-sized miracle* on Saturday morning?

Yes, catastrophic examples of human misery like hers evoke the questions that plague our minds. The little nuisances of life, even the larger travesties most of us encounter, are hardly anything compared with the unfathomably earth-shattering traumas some of our fellow human beings endure. And it is the big and shocking and devastating event that shakes us out of our complacency. That's why I've purposely selected such examples for this book.

Third, a friend who spent long hours critiquing this book manuscript for me observed, "The word that exactly describes the God you portray in this book is 'pathetic.' You have made the important point that He is not *a*pathetic; no, He experiences pathos at our pain. But it is an impotent pathos. There is little in your book of His power to deliver, or to bring good out of evil. There is only passing mention of a future where God will make all wrongs right. Thus your book tends to deprive suffering of meaning."

I respect that criticism, although I think he used the word

"pathetic" to stir me up! Because of a quirk in the English language, the expression "pathetic" goes in a very different direction than do the terms "apathetic," "sympathetic," and "empathetic." The proper adjective for God's relationship to us in our suffering is "passible" if one wishes to drop any prefix for "pathetic."

(Also, I do not see much evidence of God employing His power to deliver most of His children from their suffering. I do not doubt His power to do so, and I recognize that all of us have heard stories of miraculous deliverances from disaster, disease, and death. But I am convinced that such incidents are episodic and infrequent. And because of that, I sometimes suspect that we do others a disservice by telling these stories without balancing them with the experiences of equally sincere and dedicated people who suffer terribly right up to the moment of death. It is possible to tell "true" stories of deliverance that are not genuinely true, because they do not reflect the reality of probably more than 99 percent of the world's human population.)

However, there is another reason for not saying much about God's power to deliver or to bring good out of evil. I addressed that very aspect in the final chapter of *When God Sheds Tears* and do not want to include a lot of repetition in *When God's Heart Breaks*.

But lest anyone wonder, let me say it boldly right now: God *can* turn bad things into blessings. Romans 8:28 assures us *not* that everything that happens to us comes for our good, *but rather* that whatever happens to come our way—regardless of its intent and purpose—God can make good result from it.

We do have an active God, even though we wish we could see more obvious indications of His miraculous intervention in our lives and across the planet. The silence of God remains a difficult problem for believers.

Perhaps an extended quotation from theologian and preacher Helmut Thielicke, once rector of the University of Hamburg—the first Protestant to fill that position—and pastor of Saint Michael's Church, would be appropriate.

"The silence of God is the greatest test of our faith" *(The Silence of God, p. 12)*. He then refers to the battle of Stalingrad, which ended early in 1943. (Russia was our ally in World War II, and at Stalingrad offered fierce resistance to the Nazi forces. By the end of the five-month confrontation some 350,000 Germans had died. Add to that the Russian casualities. In fact, during World War II, more than 20 million Russian soldiers were killed or wounded. No other country sustained such drastic casualties—something most of us Americans don't know.) "What do we hear above and under its ruins? Do we not hear the roar of artillery, the tumult of the world and the cries of the dying? But where is the voice of God? When we think of God, is it not suddenly so quiet, so terribly quiet, . . . that one can hear a pin drop even though grenades are bursting around us? There is neither voice nor answer. And even if I think I hear God—hear Him in judgment . . .—He is silent again the next moment when I have to ask: Why this man, my brother or my husband?" *(ibid.,* pp. 12, 13).

But Thielicke is not done. He continues: "Men would not keep silence for so long about what is happening. They could not see so much blood shed or hear the cry of sufferers so long. Does this mean that they are more merciful [than God]?" *(ibid.,* p. 13).

He answers his own question: "Not at all! . . . They have poor nerves" *(ibid.,* pp. 13, 14). Thielicke presses on: "Obviously the silence of God is to be measured by other standards than that of men. . . . Behind the silence are His higher thoughts. . . .

"But now hear the great mystery of this silence. The very hour when God answered not a word or syllable was the hour of the great turning point when the veil of the temple was rent and God's heart was laid bare with all its wounds. Even when He was silent, God suffered with us. In His silence He experienced the fellowship of death and the depths with us. Even when we thought He did not care, or was dead, He knew all about us and behind the dark wings He did His work of love. . . .

"The silence of God and of Jesus is not of indifference. It is the silence of higher thoughts" *(ibid.,* pp. 14, 15).

Powerful words! Helpful insights.

No, our God is not pathetic—impotently wringing His hands while He suffers with us. There is more—as I brought out in *When God Sheds Tears:* "When we suffer . . . God sheds tears.

"That's comforting, but is that all God does? . . . No. Let's return to Mary, Martha, and Lazarus" (pp. 126, 127). I then describe the scene as the stone is rolled aside and Lazarus walks from the tomb. "God did more than shed tears. He beat back death.

"Jesus' whole life of miraculous ministry reveals God's intention for such matters as disaster, disease, and death. Our afflictions move God—move Him emotionally but also move Him to show His intent. We may not always see the evidence of His power today as we face tragedy—we may, instead, merely sense His tears. Nonetheless, the New Testament makes God's purposes clear.

"Ultimately God will make everything new. . . .

"And as God blots the tears from our eyes, I rather imagine He'll dab at His own eyes, too, one more time. Then the God who sheds tears will throw away His divine hanky forevermore" *(ibid.).*

Nonetheless, my friend is correct when he says that my "book tends to deprive suffering of meaning." It is because I believe that the major tragedies that mar human existence have little or no inherent meaning. They come haphazardly, are gratuitous. To see meaning in them is to justify them. Let me here repeat what I suggested in *When God Sheds Tears.* If disaster, disease, and death have some connection to the existence of sin, and if there is no explanation for sin because to explain evil is to justify it, then one concludes that disaster, disease, and death can have no meaning or justification.

Let me reemphasize. Although I do not believe that disaster, disease, and death come for the precise purpose of making us better people, that can be the result, because God—even when we think we hear nothing but His silence—can (with our cooperation) bring good out of evil. And the day is coming when disaster, disease, and death will be things of the past.

Finally, in *When God's Heart Breaks* I share with you some thoughts from where my mind and heart are now. It may be that a year or two from now I'll see things differently. But what I write here is something of an interim report. So please bear with me if you do not share exactly my perspective. What

I include here comes from both my heart and mind, but I am growing—emotionally and intellectually. That's what life is all about.

I hope that what I have written in this book will be helpful. And I hope that you'll discover it challenging, stimulating, evocative. Perhaps you will find it thought-provoking. If so, good. But I plead with you to be charitable. I have a lot more thinking to do, a lot more emoting ahead of me. Latch onto that which you find helpful. Forget about that which seems to lack usefulness. Should you disagree with me, as undoubtedly you will on occasion, care enough to think the very best anyway.

But back to the enormous tragedies that devastate our world. What do we say in the face of all this terror surrounding us and reported daily in the newspapers and other media? Sometimes silence is golden. Furthermore, I think it's safe to insist that there are some things *not* to say. Some things even as we utter them sound trite and trivial—even crass. They provide no comfort for those who are suffering, and they hardly speak well of God, who is, I continue to believe, wise, powerful, and kind. And so I hold to the concept that despite the inherent negativeness of the approach, it is indeed helpful for Christians to pause and reflect upon the ready solutions and pat answers that so glibly tumble from the tips of their tongues.

(In fact, even when our observations may be 100 percent correct, it may be the better part of wisdom to keep our comments to ourselves. Maybe it's just my personality type, but while in the throes of suffering I'd rather have you weep with me in my troubles or at least sympathize quietly with me in my loss than have to listen to your philosophical ruminations, regardless of how correct they may be. Well-intentioned defenses of God spoken even as I hurt produce resentment rather than comfort. So there are good psychological reasons as well as theological ones to bite our tongues when in the presence of sufferers.)

Because of page limitations for *When God Sheds Tears,* I

could not address all that I wished. So I take up the matter again. Perhaps another book of cautious warnings can help once more. I hope so.

## WHEN GOD'S HEART BREAKS:
*"The Lord will have compassion on Jacob"* (Isa. 14:1).

# CHAPTER ONE

## Louie, Part One

What drew us together, I really don't know—and perhaps never will.

Maybe it was because we were pretty much opposites.

Louie was tall, and I'm short. Louie sported a tan from his outside job, but I look almost peaked from my office career. He was muscular as a result of the exercise involved with his construction work, but I'm soft and flabby from having been a pastor and editor. While Louie was impetuous, I am retiring. He was quick to voice his views, but I'm timid and reserved.

Maybe it was because our wives belonged to the same small group.

As a result, my wife, Rosalia, became pretty well acquainted with Louie's wife, Heidi, whose voice was as soft and wispy as her silky blond hair.

Then again, maybe it was because our children attended the same elementary school and Sabbath school.

As a result, our Bobby and Ronny (the "by" and "ny" have long since been dropped) became friends with their T.R. and Michelle, each of whom was probably within a year of the age of our boys.

No, I still cannot say for sure just what drew Louie and me together. The roots of friendship aren't always easily discovered, are they?

❤ ❤ ❤

When both our sons decided they needed separate rooms (and who could blame them?), my wife and I asked Louie if he'd turn our garage into an extra room with a full bath. That way I could still have an office/study out there, and it would be away from the hubbub usually associated with lively youngsters.

Louie gladly accommodated us. He erected two-by-four studs. Nailing up sheetrock, he showed me how to slather on the "mud," tape the seams, and then sand it all smooth. Also he roughed out the bathroom area and installed the plumbing. When he flushed the toilet for the first time (to be sure it drained properly and had no leaks), I puzzled aloud about why steam circled up from the bowl.

The reason was quite simple, of course, and you've already guessed it. In his enthusiastic hurry Louie had hooked up the hot water to the toilet supply! But after a little additional work with his propane torch and solder, Louie had things working properly in no time at all.

Because we then had a garage door that we didn't know what to do with (Louie had taken it out and installed a large window), we decided that we needed a shed in the backyard. After all, we could hardly store our lawn tools in my office. So we asked him if he could build the shed for us.

Again, he was more than eager. The job he was then working on had plenty of leftover scraps that he could incorporate into the shed, and the supplies that were not leftovers cost us very little. But what really amazed me was the speed with which Louie constructed the shed.

Later when work slowed down for Louie and his income became pretty sparse, we again turned to him for help, thinking that we might be able to provide him with a few more needed dollars. So we asked him if he'd reshingle our house.

Of course he would! Louie told me how many flats of shingles to purchase, and I was also to order a keg of roofing nails. I selected the color of shingles for the decor of the house, and all the supplies were waiting when Louie roared up in his pickup truck.

Louie angled a long ladder against the house, and almost like a machine he began toting all those bundles of shingles to the roof. He'd toss a package of them onto his shoulder, scamper to the roof, and drop the shingles at convenient spots. When all the bundles were on the roof, he proceeded to break each one open so that he'd waste no time in applying them.

Then he promptly knocked over the open keg of nails in our gravel driveway. I spent quite a long time playing pick-up sticks (or rather pick-up nails), while Louie decided to use his air gun to affix the shingles rather than the roofing nails (that I was still hunting for with fervor).

At the end of the day, when Louie had completed the job, he discovered that we still had several packs of shingles left over. However, we could not return them for a refund because he had broken open each bundle at the outset of the job. But I didn't get upset. Why should a bundle or two of shingles ruin a friendship? Friends are too precious for that.

When Louie had finished the roof, we had one more request. Would he be willing to build a doghouse for Duchess, our German shepherd? And without any plans and with just a few scraps of lumber, Louie constructed a doghouse that lasted for some 15 years.

Once again I was astounded at his quick ability.

And you just couldn't help liking Louie. In fact, he was rather fun to have around. And although Heidi looked as though a gust of wind would whisk her away, Louie looked really solid and sturdy. And he was!

One day on one of his jobs, he was using his air gun to drive nails into the wall. Propping his left hand against the sheet rock he was installing, he operated the nail gun with his right hand. *Paroof! Paroof! Paroof!*

Suddenly Louie found it difficult to remove his left hand from the plasterboard. He had nailed the web between his left thumb and forefinger to the wall!

No problem. He put down his air gun, reached for his hammer, pried the nail from the wall, licked the trickle of blood from his wound, and was back in business. *Paroof! Paroof! Paroof!*

On another building project Louie was using the same nail

gun to install a roof. *Varoomph! Varoomph! Varoomph!* But soon his aim went awry, and Louie discovered that he had driven a nail through the top of his foot.

Again no problem. He put down his nail gun, grabbed his claw hammer, and pulled. But the nail had launched itself deep into some of the bones and stubbornly resisted his best efforts to yank it out. So he had to visit the emergency room.

After the physician had extracted the nail, he told Louie that it would be at least a week or two before he could return to work. But the next day Louie was limping around on the job!

No question about it—Louie was rugged!

Early in January of 1981 Rosalia, Bob, Ron, and I had to say goodbye to Louie, Heidi, T.R., and Michelle. We were moving to Hagerstown, Maryland, because my place of work had transferred from Nashville. We lost contact with Louie and Heidi, but once in a while we got word about them from Louie's sister and brother-in-law, who worked at the same place I did.

We learned, for example, that Louie had been working on a roof and had fallen several stories to the ground. His body took the fall with little damage, but his hands were caught in a collapsing fork lift, breaking nearly all their delicate bones.

Louie ended up losing most of his business during the long healing process. Since he couldn't use his hands very well, he applied for a rehabilitation grant. For that he had to get a medical examination. In the process of conducting the requisite physical examination, the physician thought he detected something suspicious and sent Louie for additional tests.

The results indicated that Louie had lymphoma—in stage 4. The prognosis was not very encouraging. Louie endured the usual chemotherapy and radiation therapy, but the cures didn't seem to be working very well.

About this time he was very active in an adult Bible class at church. I'm sure that it was a lively group, because Louie had opinions about almost everything—and as I said at the outset, he was not bashful about expressing them.

One day they discussed an old woman and her retarded daughter who lived in a small house in the woods. Wouldn't it be great if the class went out there and built her a porch? It would be missionary work of the most practical kind.

So one sunny Sabbath, instead of sitting in church and intellectualizing about some Bible topic, Louie and his son T.R. loaded up the pickup with lumber and screening material, Heidi and the other women made a picnic lunch, and they all drove into the woods to the place the two women called home.

By noon the deck was finished, the supports were up, and some of the screening was on. The church women laid the picnic out on the fresh new wood floor, and all joined in—adults, kids, and the two elderly women living in the house. The two women led the singing of old-fashioned hymns they remembered from childhood. They were most grateful for such a genuine display of Christian tenderness. Louie's soul, you see, was not nearly as hardened as his body.

But the Sabbath school council officials were not impressed with Louie's generosity. After all, he had led his entire Bible class in working—doing manual labor—on the Sabbath! So they reprimanded Louie because he was a commandment-breaker instead of a commandment-keeper. The Ten Commandments forbade work on Sabbath, but he and his class had indeed done work on the Lord's holy day.

Discouraged, Louie decided to look for another church to attend—a church without legalists. And he found one. Its members welcomed him, and every week held an anointing service for him.

Soon Louie swore that he had been healed as a result. In fact, he'd never felt better! He even managed to go back to work, because he had regained some use of his hands.

And what about Louie and Heidi's children?

Well, T.R. married and became a CPA, but often carried on in his father's footsteps as a builder. As Louie's health allowed, he and T.R. worked on construction projects together.

Michelle also got married—wedded her high school sweetheart, Kenny. He worked at the airport as a pilot. She took an office job and was immediately loved and respected by her fellow workers. The girl was always kind, always patient, always loving, always concerned about others.

One Sunday while Kenny was at the airport working, Michelle decided to bake a batch of cookies. The batter was pretty much mixed and just about ready for the oven when someone rapped on the apartment door.

When Michelle opened the door, she found herself confronted by a stranger who pushed his way in. This violent young man dragged her into the bedroom, ripped off her clothes, tied her up, tortured her, raped her, . . . and butchered her.

That evening when Kenny returned home, he found the brutalized body of his beautiful wife lying on their blood-soaked bed. Michelle had been dead for several hours.

Kenny phoned the police, and, as often happens, the police proceeded to consider him their chief suspect! But his alibis proved accurate, and the manhunt was on.

It wasn't until the following year that the police found the young culprit—a visitor to the area. He'd been stalking other women, and some of them had become alarmed and notified the authorities.

The young man denied any connection with Michelle's death (he lived with his aunt in the same apartment complex and was working a summer job at a fast-food place). But what he did not know was that the police had found a fingerprint in the cookie dough that Michelle had been mixing.

It was *not* hers.

It was *his!*

Also the police had run DNA tests. Again, they found confirmation. The evidence was too persuasive, too damning.

Just after Michelle's tragic death, some of Louie and Heidi's friends from their previous church phoned them.

"If Michelle hadn't gone swimming the Sabbath before, she'd still be alive," they told the grief-stricken parents.

Others informed Louie and Heidi that if only Michelle hadn't worn earrings, she wouldn't have been assaulted, tortured, raped, and murdered.

Can you fathom that? In fact, if that doesn't make your skin crawl and your blood pressure skyrocket, something is wrong with you!

Why, I believe even an atheist like Madalyn Murray O'Hair would be more sensitive than that!

You just don't tell grieving parents that if their daughter had done certain things differently, she'd still be alive.

How could they possibly know that?

Besides, that's mean-spirited! And the height of cruelty! It's ruthless! No, it's downright fiendish!

Furthermore . . . it's wrong.

What kind of God would allow a young woman to be tortured and raped and murdered because on a hot Sabbath she slipped into a bathing suit, sunned herself by the pool, and then took a quick dip in the cool water?

And what kind of God would let a young woman be brutalized beyond words and then butchered just because she dangled a pretty piece of costume jewelry from her earlobes?

Where would such a God's priorities be, for crying out loud? Is He *that* neurotic? No, that *psychotic?*

If *this* is how a loving God behaves, then who needs Him?

Drum Him out of your soul and mind!

Think for a moment, however. Exactly what would *you* have said to Louie or Heidi?

But wait! What kind of God did Jesus portray when He lived among us? After all, Jesus *was* God incarnate, we believe, so He provides us with the clearest, sharpest, and best picture of God we could possibly have.

Remember the woman caught in adultery, as related in John 8:1-11? She'd been caught red-handed—in the very act. No hearsay here. No false charges. Yet despite the gravity of her sin, Jesus treated her kindly. And without a hint of condemnation He sent her away with forgiveness marking her name and life.

*That's* the kind of God with whom we have to deal, not a peevish God who overreacts when people violate silly rules invented by neurotic religionists who are not content with what Scripture says and want to run far beyond what God actually did say.

Oh, and by the way, in 1993 Louie finally succumbed to his lymphoma and died at age 49 on the last Sabbath in February.

### WHEN GOD'S HEART BREAKS:
*"He will swallow up death forever. The Sovereign Lord will wipe away the tears from all faces" (Isa. 25:8).*

# CHAPTER TWO

## Alicia—Redemptive Value

Alicia was about four weeks away from her sixteenth birthday when Mom and Dad noticed a few lumps on her neck.

"Are you feeling OK, Alicia?"

"Yeah. Why?"

"What are those lumps?"

"What lumps?"

"On your neck."

"I don't know."

The family physician didn't know either but thought the strange lumps should receive further analysis. "It's probably Hodgkin's Disease—a kind of cancer," the doctor explained solemnly and then added with a smile, "but it looks as though we caught it in an early stage."

So Alicia underwent additional tests. They're never fun, you know, especially for a teenager.

The diagnosis came back. Alicia's affliction was not Hodgkin's. Whew!

Instead, she had lymphoma, a far more serious illness.

In January and February of 1994, Alicia checked into a children's hospital that specialized in treating cancer, and she suffered terribly from the chemotherapy. Just four weeks earlier she'd felt fine, but her chemo almost killed her. The physicians hoped that it was also killing her cancer cells.

The medical attendants thought they could detect some improvement, but suddenly a strange fungus began growing in her lungs. It took the doctors a while to figure out precisely what was causing this new distress. Alicia's grasp on life weakened.

After a long ordeal Alicia is doing better. She is now through with chemotherapy.

❤ ❤ ❤

But why has Alicia had to suffer?

Why do *innocent* people suffer?

Most of us could accept it if suffering came only upon evil-doers, but *good* people suffer. Why?

Suppose that you had to talk to Alicia. What would you tell her about her affliction? Would you tell her (or her parents, for that matter) that her lymphoma is redemptive? That's what many people would say.

You know the argument—it runs something like this: "I'm sorry you're so ill, Alicia, but remember this: God intends that your suffering be *redemptive.*"

An interesting observation, don't you think?

Now, the word "redemptive," according to the tenth edition of *Webster's Collegiate Dictionary,* means by definition to relate to or bring about "the act, process, or an instance of redeeming." That's pretty straightforward. The problem comes with the meaning of the word "redeem." You see, its nuances can embrace either the sacred or the secular.

In the religious use of the word, it means "to free from the consequences of sin" or "to atone for."

But the profane, or nonreligious, use of the expression can denote related but distinct meanings. 1. It can mean to buy back or win back—in short, to rescue. In Massachusetts, not far from where I went to college, is Redemption Rock, the place where pioneer Mary Rowlandson was freed from the Native Americans who had taken her as a prisoner during one of their forays. 2. It can also refer to the removal of an obligation or lien by payment. 3. Additionally, redeem can imply converting one thing into something else of value. You may remember the stamps that stores used to give customers for the purchases they made. I re-call my mother saving both S&H green stamps and Top Value stamps. She would go to a "redemption center" (yes, those words were on the signs in front of these places) with her booklets full of pasted-in stamps. She would exchange the stamps for a lamp or iron or some other household item. 4. Redeem can mean to fulfill or make good on, as when you might redeem stocks or bonds. 5. It can also connote offsetting the deleterious effects of something or making something worthwhile.

Were you to inform Alicia that her lymphoma was redemptive, would you have wanted to connote a religious or a secular sense? If you were using the term in a secular sense, you'd need to make clear to her just which of the five nuances you intended.

Definition 1 doesn't seem to make a lot of sense in her case, does it? What was her lymphoma buying her back from? How was her illness rescuing her—and from what? It was keeping her from having a social life with her classmates and from enjoying good health. The disease was holding her hostage, not rescuing her.

What about the second definition? How was lymphoma a payment for some obligation that Alicia had?

Maybe definition 3 is what you would mean. Was Alicia's lymphoma something she could redeem like S&H green stamps for something she would value and cherish? There may be an element of truth here. Maybe her bout with the disease taught her how to be more understanding of other sufferers. If so, then to at least some degree, her suffering was redemptive—if she came through it a better person, someone with a more desirable character or a more pleasing personality.

Then, of course, we have the fourth definition, which refers to fulfillment or making good on. I'm not quite sure just what cancer would fulfill for Alicia. Did she have some void in her life that her illness could fulfill—make complete? It surely filled the void left by her lack of poor health, because prior to her diagnosis she had enjoyed good health.

And nuance 5 seems equally puzzling to me. What harmful thing in her life was this disease offsetting or counterbalancing? What problem in her life was the lymphoma making worthwhile?

This, of course, leaves us with the religious meaning of the word "redemptive." However, we encounter a weakened nuance to this soteriological use of the term, even though it presupposes the same basic underlying definition.

When the prophet Nathan came to King David and told him a story about a wealthy man who killed a poor man's only lamb to feed his own guests, he was dealing with David in a redemptive manner, according to this weakened soteriological sense. When David did not recognize that Nathan was parodying what he himself did by having an affair with Bathsheba—having her husband killed, and then marrying her himself—but got irate over the callous behavior of the rich man and wanted him put to death, Nathan pointed his finger at David and said, "You are the man!" And David repented (2 Sam. 12).

Nathan was not, of course, David's Saviour, but he was God's agent to help facilitate the king's salvation. And God accepted David's sincere repentance for his gross behavior.

I imagine that this accommodated sense of the term is what's involved were you to tell Alicia that her lymphoma is redemptive. But another aspect immediately leaps to my mind: Redemptive for *whom*?

For Alicia?

For Mark and Karen, her parents?

For the students where she attended school?

For her local church?

For her denomination?

For the world?

I think that the person speaking would probably have it in mind that the bout with cancer would play a positive role in Alicia's salvation—in her spiritual growth as a maturing Christian.

But all this raises another more serious issue: *How is it* that Alicia's illness is redemptive?

Is she or her illness the Messiah? When I hear that someone's suffering has redeeming value, I don't think of Top Value trading stamps but of Jesus Christ. And if you're a Christian, I imagine you do the same.

An acquaintance of mine, Pastor Robert Montgomery, a Church of Christ minister and Old Testament scholar, once wrote: "Suffering can be redemptive," and he went on to de-

scribe those "who shirk all suffering. To ask them to bear the
pain of sacrifice or repentance on behalf of some higher good is
to ask the 'leopard to change his spots.' . . . They might feel
sorry for Jesus on the cross, but there is no way they are going
to join him up there, no way, no how, no time" *(Scribblings)*.

Montgomery, whom I hold in high regard, has put the issue
clearly. Those who insist that suffering is redemptive need to be
ready to join "Jesus on the cross." But most people aren't willing to follow through on what their claim entails. Instead, they
"shirk all suffering," and "there is no way they are going to join
[Jesus] up there."

Yes, when we speak of something being redemptive, our
thoughts immediately turn to Jesus Himself. As Christians we
believe that Jesus of Nazareth was the Messiah. We are convicted
that He was and is the Redeemer. And so His death on the cross
at Calvary was redemptive. That's pretty much a given for those
of us who claim to be Christians.

Paul in writing to his friend Titus spoke of "Jesus Christ, who
gave himself for us to redeem us from all wickedness" (Titus 2:14).

To the church members at Galatia, Paul asserted that "Christ
redeemed us" (Gal. 3:13). He unpacked his thoughts further by
adding: "God sent his Son, born of a woman, born under law,
to redeem those under law, that we might receive the full rights
of sons" (Gal. 4:4, 5).

The four beasts and 24 elders in Revelation, the last book of
the Bible, fell down before the Lamb—Jesus Christ—and sang:
"Thou art worthy to take the book, and to open the seals
thereof: for thou wast slain, and hast redeemed us to God by thy
blood" (Rev. 5:9, KJV).

We need to recall that earlier John the revelator had "wept
much" because "no man was found worthy to open and to read
the book" (verse 4; cf. verse 3). But the Lamb, Jesus, was worthy. Why? Because He had redeemed us. He alone was thus able
to break the seals on the scroll that John the revelator saw.

The contrast is between "no man" and Jesus—Jesus, who
alone was worthy. And why was He worthy? Because He had
died to redeem us.

We can draw only one conclusion. Jesus is the only—the sole—Redeemer. There is no other. And surely all of us believe this.

As a result, Christians have insisted throughout history that it is rank heresy to suggest that Jesus' work as our Redeemer was somehow insufficient and needs to be supplemented by something that we do. Yet I feel uneasy when someone tells a sufferer that his or her suffering is to be redemptive. I wonder if it might be understood to mean that the disease is somehow complementing what Jesus has already done.

We have come, then, to the very core of Christian belief. Christians may differ on many things. We may argue over Jesus' incarnate nature or bicker over whether He is *homoiousios* or *homoousios* (the same *as* God or *like* God). Or we may dispute the role of law in religion. But Christians don't fight over the adequacy of Jesus' sacrifice on Calvary. He died once and for all (Heb. 9:12). His "single" sacrifice was "for all time" (Heb. 10:12, 14, NRSV).

And I think we would all be better off as we use the word "redemptive" in its religious sense to employ it cautiously and precisely. When we say that something is redemptive in this spiritual context, we want to be clear as to how something is redemptive and why and for whom.

❤ ❤ ❤

So what about Alicia?

Obviously, she can't do a single thing to augment her redemption, her salvation. She can't do a solitary thing to augment her parents' salvation or that of her classmates. Nor can she add anything to augment her church's salvation or the world's.

Alicia isn't a redeemer. Jesus alone is.

Alicia isn't a savior. Jesus Himself, and no other, is.

We all agree with that. But what about her lymphoma? Can it make Alicia a more sensitive and thoughtful person? It surely has that potential, but it doesn't automatically have to. And if that is what we mean when we use the word "redemptive," then we're back to its secular usage. Just as S&H green stamps had no inherent value but could result in my mother getting something of value when she "redeemed" them at a "redemption center," so in this same secular sense Alicia's lymphoma, which surely had no value, could help her build a more positive character, but then so can doing chores around the house, caring for the infirmed, or a thousand other activities.

And what about the soteriological or religious sense of the word? I dare say that Alicia's suffering is *not* redemptive.

What, then, of Alicia?

She's an unfortunate victim.

She's suffered greatly.

In fact, what she's gone through, no teen should have to endure.

Her plight is tragic . . . and sad . . . and reprehensible. But it is *not* redemptive.

Perhaps it would be better to remind Alicia of her Redeemer, who loves her unfailingly and is always compassionate and whose redemptive work will someday utterly destroy the tragedies that plague human existence.

### WHEN GOD'S HEART BREAKS:

*"Yet the Lord longs to be gracious to you; he rises to show you compassion. . . . You will weep no more" (Isa. 30:18, 19).*

# CHAPTER THREE

## Samantha—Good in Itself

The place—Pittsburgh, Pennsylvania. The date—August 14, 1993. You may have read about it in your local newspaper. Here's what my newspaper reported *(Morning Herald,* Sept. 1, 1993, p. B4).

Twenty-one-year-old Steven Lytle was playing the Nintendo video game Terminator 2. *Plinkety plunk. Clackety clack. Clinkety clank. Bang. Boom. Ta-ta-ta-ta.* It sure was a lot of fun, but his 3-month-old daughter, Samantha, was fussing, making him lose concentration. And when you lose concentration, you lose the game.

So Daddy stomped over to the crib where tiny Samantha lay and punched her in the head several times. He then returned to the video game, playing it for another hour.

When Steven checked his watch again, he decided that he might better look in on little Samantha. But when he peeked into her crib, he discovered blood pouring from her ears.

Quickly he dialed 9-1-1.

Within minutes the ambulance arrived, and the paramedics rushed Samantha to Children's Hospital, where she was pronounced DOA. In case you might have forgotten, that means dead on arrival!

Detective Gary Tallent said Steve Lytle admitted that "he had problems with his daughter at times. He said he punched her in the stomach about a month ago."

Punched 2-month-old Samantha in the stomach? Socked 3-month-old Samantha in the head? Yes, indeedy!

Now back to Terminator 2! *Plinkety plunk. Clackety clack. Clinkety clank. Bang. Boom. Ta-ta-ta-ta.*

Let's see, now. What would you tell Samantha, if you could? What would you have cooed to her as blood seeped from her ears and life ebbed from her tiny body? Would you tell her, as some people insist, that suffering in and of itself is really somehow inherently good?

My Church of Christ pastor friend, Robert Montgomery, whom I cited in the previous chapter, likewise mentioned this argument in his *Scribblings*: "There is a current that runs through our society that argues that pain is good, almost exclusively good. . . . In short, those who suffer ought to be glad for their suffering itself. And the rest of us can do them a favor by leaving them in it."

What about this idea?

The notion that suffering is inherently good in and of itself is the underpinning of asceticism. And many sincere men and women have bought into the idea and have tortured their bodies and minds because of it.

Not all of them have been Christians, either. Asceticism appears in many, if not most, religions.

The word "asceticism" comes from Greek and originally described the lifestyle of athletes, who trained arduously and ate sparingly.

Anthony, a Christian born in Koma, Egypt, around A.D. 250, invented Christian monasticism. He lived in luxury until he was about 20 years old, when he read Jesus' words to the rich young ruler: "If you wish to be perfect, go, sell your possessions, and give the money to the poor, and you will have treasure in heaven" (Matt. 19:21, NRSV). Immediately Anthony began living in poverty in his own village, having given away all his riches.

About A.D. 285 he decided that his privation was not sufficient, so he located an isolated tomb and lived there. After 15 years, he concluded that he wanted further isolation, so he took up residence in an abandoned castle on Mount Pispir, not far from the Nile River. Here he lived for some 20 years before seeking even deeper solitude near the Red Sea, where he remained for the rest of his life.

Anthony fasted and prayed. He tormented his body in order to keep it in submission. During his frequent fasts, he felt that the devil came to torment him, sometimes appearing in the guise of a soldier, sometimes looking like a woman, and at other times taking on the form of wild beasts. Anthony would do physical battle with the visitors and come away bruised and battered. "Those who witnessed them [these 'many such attacks'] were convinced they were real" *(Encyclopaedia Britannica,* vol. 1, p. 444).

Anthony died on January 17, 356—a very old man.

Simeon Stylites was probably the most famous Christian ascetic. Also known as Simeon the Elder, he was born around A.D. 390 in the town of Sisan, which was located in Cilicia. Initially he cared for sheep, and he stepped inside a church for the first time in his life when he was 13 years old. At that point he decided that he should become a monk. Simeon proceeded to join a monastery, but the order sent him packing because he was too ascetic even for them!

He moved to a site northwest of Aleppo, and from A.D. 423 until his death in 459, he existed on the top of a tall pole. At first the column was only six feet tall, but gradually Simeon had it built higher, until it stood more than 50 feet high. Atop the pole, Simeon was exposed to all the elements. He slept standing up as he leaned against the railing circling the top of the column. His admirers climbed a ladder to provide him with food and water.

Before long Simeon's place of vigil became a tourist attraction, with pilgrims making long treks so that they could see and admire the saintly man. Because of the public attention that Simeon drew, "he was a powerful factor in promoting peace" *(New Schaff-Herzog Encyclopedia of Religious Knowledge,* vol. 11, p. 123). And following his death, other devout men took up a similar lifestyle, among them Saint Daniel (A.D. 409-493); Saint Simeon Stylites the Younger (A.D. 517-592); Saint Alypius (seventh century), who perched atop a pillar for 67 years; Saint Luke (A.D. 879-979); Saint Lazarus (A.D. 968-1054); and Saint Wulflaicus.

Heinrich Suso, or Seuse, was born March 21, 1295 or 1300—authorities cannot agree on the precise year. Born into a noble family, he had a keen mind. He joined the Dominican order when he was only 13, but he felt that his spiritual life there was lacking. When he went to study under Meister Eckhart, his ascetic tendencies got refined.

Ultimately Heinrich Suso manufactured and wore a hair shirt lined with straps studded with metal points and needles. He also used to whip himself until he bled. His diet was sparse, and he lived in almost total isolation for many years.

Finally, when he was 40 years of age, he had to give up his ascetic practices because, unlike the Stylites (the name had come to refer to other "pillar saints"), most of whom were long-lived, they had been slowly but surely killing him. His health then rallied, and he lived some 25 to 30 years more.

One of the most famous and more recent non-Christian ascetics was Mohandas (Mahatma) Gandhi. He accomplished more by his austere lifestyle and periodic fasts than any army could.

But there's another aspect to the idea that suffering is good. Perhaps you have heard the following story, which has been gaining popularity among Christians in recent years, probably (I suspect) because of the pervasiveness of New Age thinking even on those who would be shocked to be identified with it.

An old Chinese man, who was something of a philosopher, had a horse and a son. One day the horse disappeared, and his neighbors came by to console him. "What a bad thing to happen!" they said.

But the old man responded, "But how do you know it's bad?"

A week or two later the horse returned but was not alone. With it was another horse. And the old man's friends stopped by to congratulate him on the good luck he'd had. "But how do you know it's good?" he asked.

One day when the man's only son was out trying to break

the new horse, the ungrateful beast threw the lad, who broke his leg upon hitting the ground. Again the neighbors stopped by to commiserate with the old man. "What a bad thing has happened," they bemoaned.

"But how do you know it's bad?" he replied.

Then came word that the local warlord was forming an army of all able-bodied young men, but because the old man's son had a broken leg, he was not impressed into the military. Once again the neighbors stopped by to celebrate the man's good fortune, and once again the old man answered, "But how do you know . . ."

Those who tell this intriguing story in the context of suffering usually like to nail their point home by reemphasizing that we simply are not in any position to decide whether a given event is either good or bad. All that we can truly determine is whether or not things are painful or pleasant. More about this later.

If when evangelical Christians relate this old story today they simply mean that God can bring good things out of bad situations, then I agree with them. God *can* take the terrible things that happen to us and help us cope in such a way that we grow spiritually and become better men and women as a result. And maybe that is all most people want to infer from the story. (True as it is, even this observation is not particularly helpful to the person in the throes of suffering, and most of the time it is better left unsaid.)

However, I find the account troubling because of its mystic overtones. And although those who tell the story do not generally ascribe to ancient Chinese Taoism, that's where the story has its roots. Now, it is true that an idea or even a practice need not be tainted simply because of its ancient origin in, say, paganism. Most of the time the concept or practice has become so worn with age that its original meaning is no longer discernible. For example, the practice of having bridesmaids and groomsmen at a wedding has become conventional and does not mean that the bride and groom have asked these people to join them so that the devil will be confused as to the identity of the real bride and groom and therefore cannot put a curse on their marriage—the original purpose for having attendants at a wedding.

But this particular story is not, to my way of thinking, that far removed from its original context. When my friend Kevin heard the story, he immediately spoke of yin and yang (ancient Chinese mystical concepts devolving from a philosophy known as monism) and said that when something good happens to him, he immediately wonders when something bad will occur—or vice versa.

A second point that sincere and devoted Christians often make is that in the light of eternity, what happens here during our "threescore and ten" years pales into inconsequence. Relatively speaking, what are 70 or 80 years in comparison (or should we say in contrast) with 100,000 years or 1 million years, which themselves are just a fraction of eternity? Similarly, of what consequence are our physical experiences when compared with spiritual matters? Or of what importance are earthly matters in light of heavenly things?

While again such an observation has a large element of truth—and I suspect that all of us will feel that way when we live forever in heaven—I want to counter by suggesting that regardless of how weighty spiritual and eternal matters are, the fact is that what we know and have to deal with during our 70 or 80 or 100 years of life here and now *is* material and earthly. We cannot see heaven or hear spiritual matters. Nor can we taste eternity, touch God, or smell forever.

One might respond with "That's not true. In Hebrews 11 we read about those great men and women of faith who, with Abraham, looked for a 'city . . . whose builder and maker is God' [verse 10, KJV]. 'They were longing for a better country—a heavenly one' [verse 16]. Like Moses they endure, 'as seeing him who is invisible' [verse 27, KJV]. That's what faith is all about. It is 'the evidence of things not seen' [verse 1, KJV]."

Now, I agree that Christians should not fall into crass materialism. Aside from the conclusions of reason and the evidence of our senses, we should also give serious consideration to faith. Since we believe that there truly is a spiritual realm—a God and a heaven, for example—that belief should make a difference in our lives. But the point is that not only can we live with a focus away from material things to spiritual matters, but that doing this is eminently desirable. Indeed, this is how the great saints of the Old Testament lived, according to the New Testament Epistle to the Hebrews. Again, more about this later.

Why, then, do I find aspects of these arguments disconcerting? The basis for Christian asceticism has roots deep in ancient Iranian religion and later Middle Platonic philosophy (which in turn, of course, built upon earlier Platonic thought). Later it found rebirth in a Judaeo-Christian heresy that came to be known as Gnosticism. Although the onset of Gnosticism proper remains hidden in obscurity, early Church Fathers insisted that Simon Magus, mentioned in the biblical book of Acts, was its founder. "The first certain early Christian reference to the term . . . is 1 Tim 6:20" *(Anchor Bible Dictionary,* vol. 2, p. 1033).

Part of Gnostic theology insisted that "the world, produced from evil matter and possessed by evil demons, cannot be a creation of a good God" *(Encyclopaedia Britannica,* vol. 5, p. 315). Instead, this material world in which we live came into being through the demiurge, whom they called a "foolish creator." Accordingly, Gnostics regarded anything connected with matter, especially the body, as inherently bad.

Through the process of gaining revealed light or knowledge (*gnōsis* in Greek), "the gnostics understood themselves to be the elite 'chosen people' " and could embark on a life of illumination that would help them "be freed from the fetters of this world (spirit from matter, light from darkness)" *(ibid.,* vol. 2, p. 1033). This view, then, saw salvation as "not a matter of deliverance from sin and guilt . . . but of the freeing of the spirit from matter . . . , in particular, the material human body" *(ibid.,* p. 1034).

Their disregard of things material, especially the human body, led to extreme ascetic practices, because the body was inherently evil, having been constructed by the "foolish creator," and so it needed to be kept in abasement and neglect. As a result, deprivation and pain would come to be seen as good because of their important role in freeing the human soul or spirit from imprisonment to the body consisting of evil matter.

Gnosticism posed an extremely serious threat to Christianity, and although the Church Fathers wrote polemics against it, soon Gnostic influence even permeated orthodox Christianity through the monastic ideal. Quickly ascetic practitioners embraced celibacy, abstemiousness, fasting, lack of personal hygiene, introspection that produced mental and emotional anguish, physical discomfort, and even self-inflicted pain.

Well, is it true that most of us have it all wrong? Were Anthony, Simeon Stylites the Elder, Simeon Stylites the Younger, Alypius, Wulflaicus, Heinrich Suso, and Gandhi right? And what about the world's great mystics such as Bernard of Clairvaux, Meister Eckhart, Saint Francis of Assisi, Jakob Böhme, Buddha, Lao-tzu, Abu Yazid, Johannes Tauler, Jalal-ud-din Rumi, and others?

Maybe it's time to return to that story about the Chinese farmer.

First, let's discuss the man's philosophy. It is not by accident that he is Chinese, because his words reflect a kind of Asian mysticism in which all is one (monism, philosophers call it) and so must be seen as a whole. Thus we must not focus on the parts but on the whole, because all is one—black *and* white, good *and* bad, yin *and* yang. And because all is one, it is impossible in such a wholistic view of life to distinguish one from the other. Something may appear to be bad, but it is really more accurate to say that it is inconvenient, because every coin has two sides. What we may regard as a nuisance may end up being either good or bad, but who knows?

I also find it surprising that such a philosophy and story closely resemble what I have read in the book *Beyond Illness,* by Larry Dossey. The author, a physician in Texas, puts forward a philosophy of health and illness strongly shaped by Buddhist, Hindu, Taoist, and New Age thought.

Dr. Dossey accepts a monism in which health and illness are

practically indistinguishable. "Health and illness come together in harmonious perfection," he insists (p. 45). He goes so far as to argue that "absolute distinctions between health and illness are illusions" *(ibid.)*. As a consequence, according to Dr. Dossey, if we were successful somehow in doing away with all illness, we would at the same time also eliminate all health *(ibid., p. 47)*. So Dr. Dossey can speak of "the *necessity* of disease" *(ibid., p. 49)*. Why is illness necessary? Because without it we would be unable to know health.

As he continues his discussion, Dr. Dossey asserts that pain and death belong, because they are not unnatural and are not "foreign intruders" *(ibid., pp. 81, 82)*. Rather, they are interconnected *(ibid., p. 96)*. He compares them to music: "Like counterpoint in music, sickness and health exist as two melodic parts to life intended to be heard simultaneously" *(ibid., p. 118)*.

And so he can aver that "illness . . . leads health onward, . . . is its progenitor, its guarantor" *(ibid., p. 124)*. "Health and illness *are* one" *(ibid., p. 142)*.

The bottom line is this, according to Dr. Dossey: "Healing becomes impossible" *(ibid., p. 134)*. "At the deepest level the sick person has no sickness" *(ibid., p. 135)*. So "health exists as a state which cannot be sundered by the appearance of cancer nor the eruption of a heart attack. It [health] is a ground state, a state of wholeness which excludes nothing" *(ibid., pp. 179, 180)*. Thus "longevity, absence of pain and suffering, and illness are *inconsequential* to health" *(ibid., p. 185; italics supplied)*. Note that word again, the same word some evangelical Christians use of life's ups and downs.

The fact is that that philosophy has had a number of definitions of what is truly real. One school of philosophy has its roots in the ruminations of Plato and later Aristotle. Unfortunately, this school of thought goes by two different philosophical terms—idealism and realism. And the two terms can be applied to two completely different (and opposing) schools of thought!

In this chapter we'll stick with the term *idealism,* because it reflects Plato's emphasis on the highest reality, which he called in Greek *idea* or *ideal.* The logical conclusions of this school of thinking later erupted in both Christianity and Judaism in Gnostic thought.

According to idealism, the real does not exist here on earth but solely in heaven. The things we know here on our planet are mere shadows of reality. The real chair, for example, exists in heaven. What we sit on is a shadow of that reality. Philosophers must come to the place where they no longer focus on the shadows but rather on the reality. We must concentrate, according to idealism, on the spiritual world rather than the materialistic world, because the material world is of no consequence. It is unreality.

And according to the Gnostic conclusion, this material world was, therefore, not created by the good and true God but by an evil Demiurge who is responsible for all that is material.

Now, based on this line of thinking, "philosophical theism is an idealist view, for according to theism God is a perfect, uncreated spirit who has created everything else and is hence more fundamental in the world than any material things he has created" (*Encyclopedia of Philosophy*, vol. 4, p. 110).

If that is the case, then all Christians are idealists (belong to the philosophical school of thought known as idealism), because they believe in God. However, typical Christian theism (the doctrine of believing in God) is a rather watered-down idealism. A more stringent idealism is pantheism, which "may be regarded as a more thoroughly idealist view than theism, since pantheism is the view that nothing exists except God and his modes and attributes, so that the material world must be an aspect or appearance of God" (*ibid.*).

Idealism itself breaks up into several schools, but all idealists would insist, among other things, that universals exist (the really real, which is not material); that the really real actually transcends the here and now; that we should use a dialectical approach in our thinking by which the bad can be transcended to produce good or that we must keep in tension such opposites as good and bad, black and white, yin and yang; and that mind is superior to matter (see *Encyclopaedia Britannica*, vol. 6, p. 240).

Idealism holds that "reality reveals its ultimate nature more faithfully in its highest qualities (mental) than in its lowest (ma-

terial)" *(ibid.,* vol. 25, p. 626). And according to Baruch
Spinoza, idealists "strive to view the contemporary world 'under
the aspect of eternity'" *(ibid.,* p. 627). As a result, "nearly all
Idealists accept the principle that the evils with which man has
to deal may become ingredients in a larger whole that overcomes
them" *(ibid.).*

That is the core of philosophical idealism, and "similar doc-
trines have played central roles in Indian, Chinese, and Islamic
metaphysics and epistemology" *(ibid.,* vol. 6, p. 240).

Materialism, however, takes the opposite approach. Reality
exists only in this material world. There is no real spiritual realm
at all. Matter is all that matters, and we should concentrate on
that which is real—matter. And philosophical empiricism insists
that what is truly real is that which we can somehow detect with
our five physical senses.

If you have been following this somewhat technical discussion of idealism, you have probably felt that some of the time
you were an idealist but that other times you probably concluded that you are not an idealist.

Yes, you believe in spiritual reality—the reality of heaven and
eternity. Nonetheless, you really know nothing much about
eternity since all you experience is the past, present, and the future when it becomes the present. Immersed in time, you can
hardly fathom what "eternity" or "eternal things" really means.

Also you have suffered. Bad things have happened to you.
Headaches and toothaches have tormented you, and you've bit-
ten your tongue. Friends and relatives have died—some after
long periods of unremitted suffering. You've visited hospital
rooms and read about crack babies. On TV you've seen the effects of war and famine and airplane crashes and mudslides and
floods and droughts. And it's almost impossible for you to keep
these realities balanced with their allegedly flipside of benefi-
cence. It's not easy for you to admit that the most dastardly,
most tragic, most disastrous, most catastrophic, most devastating elements of life are simply pesky annoyances.

And although you admit that God is real and is the Creator
of all, you most likely have to admit that on a day-to-day basis

He is not as immediate to you as are potatoes, carrots, shirts, skirts, cars, paper, computers, and paychecks, despite the fact that you pray to Him many times throughout the day.

I'd like to suggest that *both* the material world *and* the spiritual realm are real. It is not that one is real and the other is not. Nor is it even that one is more real than the other. (I don't know how anything can be more real than something else. Surely, something is either real or it is not.) But what says that reality must be always the same? that there cannot be distinctions between reality? that there cannot be different kinds of reality?

Furthermore, even if we grant that spiritual things (heaven, for example) are also real, the fact of the matter is that despite our belief in them, on an everyday basis all we have to deal with is the material because we are material beings who gather our knowledge (of other material things) via our senses. We bathe our material bodies, wear our material clothing, eat our material foods, work at our material jobs, and deal with other material beings. In no way can we get away from our material existence.

And since this material world is all that our senses can detect, it is what is truly real to us today—irrespective of our religious beliefs. Abraham and Moses may have looked for an immaterial city and lived as seeing what is invisible, but they too were very much immersed in this material world. Let me repeat what I said earlier: We cannot see God, smell the tree of life, hear heaven, taste the Holy City, or touch eternity. These things that we cannot sense remain "theoretical constructs" (another philosophical term)—ideas, thoughts, imaginings, concepts of what may indeed be real—but they are not the things that impact us 24 hours of every day.

Even the most ardent ascetic still focused on material things—scratchy hair shirts reinforced with metallic points, self-flagellation to draw blood with whips, a sparse diet that left one with hunger pangs, little to drink so that one was nearly dehydrated, shivering with goose bumps because of exposure to cold weather, fighting yawns and fatigue because of almost no sleep. Yes, in the name of spirituality, they were quite materialistically focused!

For those of us who take Scripture very seriously, we should realize that the story of the Chinese man and his insistence that material life is of little consequence fly in the face of the Hebrew Scriptures, which strongly affirmed this world. The Old Testament emphasizes that God—the God who is goodness personified and who Himself is the definition of goodness—created a world that He kept calling good after each day of Creation week. Additionally, Genesis insists that human beings were created in the very image of God—the benevolent and perfect Creator Himself.

Because of this foundational theological presupposition, the ancient Hebrew religion was very much world-affirming. The psalmist could sing about the earth and proclaim it as belonging to the Lord. And in the closing chapters of the book of Job, the Creator Himself speaks fondly of His material creation, proudly pointing to the foundation of the earth, the sea, the rain and hail and snow, the lion, the raven, the mountain goat, the ass, the ox, the ostrich, the horse, and the hawk.

As a result, "Judaism, because of its view that God created the world and that the world (including man) is good, is nonascetic in character" *(Encyclopaedia Britannica,* vol. 1, p. 617).

It was only as developing Judaism itself became influenced by Zoroastrian dualism and Platonic thought that it could begin spawning such ascetic anomalies as the Essenes, commonly thought to have lived at Qumran, among other places, and mystic anomalies as well.

The end result of this mystical/ascetic speculation is that it trivializes both the real material world around us and the terrible impact of disaster, disease, and death.

So let's return to little Samantha. Is it true that her death was not bad? That her untimely death was really good? Or maybe simply a nuisance, something like a mosquito bite? Or inconsequential in the light of eternity?

Are our instincts *that* botched up? Are we so deceived that we perceive Samantha's death as bad when it really is good in and of itself? Little wonder that G. van der Leeuw, renowned student of world religions, has observed: "[Mysticism] is a form . . . of autism" *(Religion in Essence and Manifestation,* vol. 2, p. 507). He refers, of course, to a kind of spiritual autism, a withdrawal or splitting off from reality.

If we buy into this philosophy that suffering is somehow not bad, as we usually assume, but inherently good (or at least of little consequence), then it seems to me that something is seriously wrong with our sense of moral value.

Now, I want to be the first to admit in all candor that I think people today have a crazy, mixed-up value system. I suspect that most contemporary people are not as morally acute as they should be. In fact, I'll go even further and suggest that all of us have had our moral sensibilities blunted. You need only listen to the news on the radio or watch it on TV or read it in the newspapers and weekly news magazines to know that something is drastically wrong with our sense of moral values.

Lives are snuffed out every day. We perpetrate on our fellow human beings terrible atrocities. Think of Ireland. Think of Sarajevo. Think of South Africa. Think of Israel. Think of Florida. Think of Washington, D.C. Think of Los Angeles. Think of Bosnia. Think of Haiti. Think of your own local town! Is your community immune from the evils of crime?

June Strong, in her delightful book *A Warm and Welcome Place,* refers to a letter someone sent to *People* magazine. "I was astonished," wrote the reader, "to see what is essentially an archaic religious concern (i.e., 'sin'), appropriate and consequential only to the Pilgrims or the Bible, on the pages of *People.* . . . To me the phrase 'It's a sin' became strictly a slang expression years ago" (p. 25).

Really, now! "It's a sin" is merely a slang expression?

Then what word does this reader use to categorize rape and robbery and murder and kidnapping and lying and adultery and molestation?

If a majority of Americans agree with this writer, then no

wonder we have such a slimy moral morass in our country today!

Sin is *not* a slang word. Evil is *not* a colloquialism.

It boggles my mind by what process of reasoning one can conclude that disaster, disease, and death are good (or merely nuisances) in and of themselves—and not the bane, the scourge, the blight, the calamity, the adversity, the affliction, the catastrophe, the curse, yes, *the evil* that we normally think they are.

"Woe unto them," Isaiah proclaimed, "that call evil good, and good evil; that put darkness for light, and light for darkness; that put bitter for sweet, and sweet for bitter! Woe unto them that are wise in their own eyes" (Isa. 5:20, 21, KJV).

The Hebrew word behind "good" here is *tov,* and the Hebrew word translated "evil" is *raʿ.* Generic terms, they not only can refer to moral good and evil but can also denote something less fraught with moral overtones. *Tov,* for example, can also mean beneficial, favorable, lovely, cheerful, comfortable, delightful, and even fruitful. It functions pretty much as our generic word "good." Similarly, *raʿ* can describe that which is broken, spoiled, of inferior quality, and adverse. It, too, functions pretty much like our word "bad."

So we need not insist that Isaiah's words are limited to people who confuse sin with righteousness, moral evil with moral good. His metaphor that follows (bitter and sweet) really need not have moral overtones, so we probably are not doing him an injustice if we apply his words to anyone who has trouble differentiating between beneficial and adverse, delightful and inferior, comfortable and broken.

I know my emphasis here is strong, but I suspect that all too many of those who suggest that suffering is not evil but is good in and of itself have something broken inside their heads—and hearts. Somehow their value system has become botched up.

But consider yet another point—one with terrible practical implications. Why should we try to alleviate that which is good in and of itself? Surely we must not oppose that which is good!

So maybe we should rejoice that 3-month-old Samantha's daddy punched her in the stomach and head.

Of course! Isn't that what good daddies around the world do

to their children—punch them in the head so that blood pours from their ears and so that they arrive at the hospital DOA?

Yes, what a blessing it was for Samantha to have Steve Lytle as her father!

No.

I simply cannot buy it.

In my view, disaster, disease, and death are not good in and of themselves. If they were intrinsically good, then we would expect to find them adding to the bliss of heaven. But that is not the kind of paradise we discover in the book of Revelation. There we read: "He will wipe every tear from their eyes. There will be no more death or mourning or crying or pain, for the old order of things has passed away" (Rev. 21:4).

And they are, I believe, more than an inconvenience along life's road. They are not something we can ignore during our lifetimes simply because we're religious and believe that spiritual realities can be just as real as material realities, especially in the light of eternity. We are not eternal beings and know little or nothing about the nature of eternity. All we know about is the passing of time—past, present, and future.

To my way of thinking, disaster, disease, and death are evil. And we must not do or say anything that tends to trivialize them. They are the result of sin. Let us get our sense of values straight!

Perhaps it might be better to tell Samantha that what her daddy did to her was terribly evil. That good daddies don't punch their kids in the head or stomach. But there is a Father who is never evil and who loves her more than we can ever understand. And He will always cherish her and hold her close.

### WHEN GOD'S HEART BREAKS:
*"He tends his flock like a shepherd: He gathers the lambs in his arms and carries them close to his heart; he gently leads those that have young" (Isa. 40:11).*

# CHAPTER FOUR

## Bill—In a Prior Life

Seven-foot-tall, 300-pound Bill Simpson was nicknamed "Big Tiny" by his friends. You may have read about him in the news magazines or newspapers or perhaps saw his story on television. Bill gained instant fame back in August and September of 1993 because he lived in Vidor, Texas—the sole Black man living in an all-White neighborhood.

Despite his size, people often referred to Bill as a gentle giant, and both friends and the police described him as a "teddy bear." But the Ku Klux Klan didn't appreciate someone like Bill Simpson darkening lily-white Vidor, and they made their hatred known in numerous ways.

Finally Bill Simpson could take the stress no longer. "I was tired of worrying about who might do something, when, and if they came, how many," he said.

So when Lin-Marie Garsee—a White woman—of Beaumont, Texas, a few miles distant, heard of his plight, she offered to rent a diminutive house to the enormous Bill Simpson. Despite its size, the new house sure looked good to Mr. Simpson. It was almost as though Bill put on the house rather than lived in it—he was so large and the house so tiny.

But 12 hours after moving in, Bill Simpson, the gentle Black giant, was dead on the streets of Beaumont.

And not from the KKK, either.

On Wednesday, September 1, 1993, at 10:30 p.m. Michael Wayne Zeno—a 19-year-old Black man affiliated with the Los

Angeles-based Crips gang—pumped five bullets into Bill Simpson, killing him almost instantly. Police also looked for three other accomplices.

"I have cried and cried and cried," commented Lin-Marie Garsee. "When Bill left here yesterday, he said 'Lin-Marie, I'm finally home.' He called me his guardian angel—but I don't feel like much of a hero today" *(USA Today,* Sept. 3, 1993, p. 3A).

What was this gentle giant's problem?

Some people, influenced by Eastern religious thought, would tell us that Bill Simpson got what was coming to him— not because he was a bad person in Texas, for he wasn't, but because in a previous life he had not lived uprightly. Now in his reincarnated life as Bill Simpson, he got what was his due.

This idea is gaining in popularity all the time. Most of us have heard (or read) about individuals who, under hypnosis, have spoken as though they had lived at least one life prior to their present one. Allegedly, they relate details about some person in the past whom they would not have known about from usual means. So the conclusion that many jump to is that such individuals provide living documentation for reincarnation.

What about it?

Did Mr. Simpson get what was coming to him because of his evil deeds from a past existence? How would *you* respond?

Christians do not generally accept the philosophy of reincarnation, but many Christians do believe in the immortality of the soul and consider it a fundamental Christian doctrine. Those who believe that the soul is inherently immortal and so does not and cannot die might find reincarnation a relatively difficult concept to combat. Their arguments against it often have to rely on scriptural silence. And arguments from silence may be right, but they can just as easily be wrong. Logicians warn against using or believing arguments from silence. Just because a person does not address a specific issue does not mean that he or she is either for it or against it—even when that individual may be speaking of related issues. One does not usually say all that one thinks on a given issue at any specific time or place.

So when Christians argue that because the Bible does *not* say anything about living previous lives and reincarnation there is, therefore, no such thing as reincarnation because no one has lived a previous life, they may well be correct. But their insistence does not rest on sound argumentation.

The traditional Christian understanding that believers do not truly die but that death merely opens the door to another level of existence for the deceased (one in the perfect bliss of heaven with God and the angels) logically leaves such Christians open to the possibility of reincarnation. If in the future, upon death, people live on, why not extend life in the opposite direction and believe that people existed in the past prior to their contemporary existence? There appear to be no logical brakes to keep the popular Christian belief from sliding backward into the past.

However, a significant body of Christian thinkers do not have this problem. They believe that each person is a whole—and that each person *is* a soul rather than *has* a soul. The distinction between the verbs "is" and "has" is critical for these thinkers. The former speaks of one's nature, the latter of one's possessions.

It is an important insight, one we should not underestimate. The wholistic understanding of the psychosomatic unity of each human being is accepted by a growing number of scholars and theologians and is a tenet, for example, of Seventh-day Adventist fundamental beliefs. According to this perspective, when a person dies nothing lives on. And such Christians refer to an array of biblical passages to back them up.

Although this perspective on human nature and what happens at death appears to fly in the face of what traditional Christianity has taught, that is not necessarily the case. Many both historical and contemporary Christian thinkers insist that human beings are whole creatures and are not made up of different parts, such as body and soul. They also remind us that human beings are not inherently immortal and so do not have an immortal soul, contrary to popular Christian thought.

Among the Apostolic Fathers, Clement of Rome, Ignatius of Antioch, Barnabas of Alexandria, Hermas of Rome, and

Polycarp of Smyrna espoused this biblical concept. Also it found support in the Didachē and the Epistle to Diognetus. Additionally, about half the Ante-Nicene Fathers held the same basic Christian doctrine: Justin Martyr, Tatian, Theophilus of Antioch, Melito of Sardis, Polycrates of Ephesus, Irenaeus, Novatian of Rome, and Arnobius of Sicca. The Clementine Homilies put forth a similar doctrine.

Martin Luther spoke of death as a sleep. "For the human soul sleeps with all senses buried, and our bed is like a sepulcher. . . . Thus, the place of the dead has no torments. Our death and resurrection will also be like this" *(Luther: Works, Eight Lectures on Genesis 45-50,* p. 318).

John Milton, the great Christian poet of the seventeenth century, wrote: "The death of the body as it is called is the loss or extinction of life. For the separation of body and soul, which is the usual definition of death, cannot possibly be death at all. . . . So far I have proved that the whole man dies" *(Two Books of Investigations Into the Christian Doctrine Drawn From the Sacred Scriptures Alone,* Vol. I, p. 13).

Renowned theologian Oscar Cullmann commented on the immortality of the soul: "This widely-accepted idea is one of the greatest misunderstandings of Christianity" *(Immortality of the Soul or Resurrection of the Dead?,* p. 15), because "the Jewish and Christian interpretation of creation excludes the whole Greek dualism of body and soul" *(ibid.,* p. 30).

Christopher Allison has observed: "Another important but less well known fact about Christianity is the crucial difference between 'resurrection of the body' and 'immortality of the soul.' The latter is not the Hebraic and biblical belief but a part of Greek Platonic thought that had a very large influence on the church as it spread through the Greek-speaking world. Christianity does not have a belief in some separate indestructible part of man called a psychē or soul. There is nothing way down in man that is essentially and innately indestructible" *(Guilt, Anger, and God,* p. 99).

Lutheran New Testament scholar Krister Stendahl has pointed out that "the question about the immortality of the soul is interesting for someone who is primarily a Biblical scholar because he specializes in sixty-six so-called books that do not know of immortality of the soul." Instead, "the whole world which comes to us through the Bible . . . is not interested in the immortality of the soul. And if you think it is, it is because you have read it into the material" *(Metanoia,* p. 3).

Clark H. Pinnock, an influential evangelical theologian, has called the concept of the immortality of the soul "unbiblical anthropology" *(Four Views on Hell,* p. 147). He points out that this unbiblical anthropology has its roots in Plato's philosophical ruminations. Pinnock then boldly states: "The Bible does not teach the natural immortality of the soul; it points instead to the resurrection of the body as God's gift to believers. . . . The Bible teaches conditionalism; God created humans mortal with a capacity for life everlasting, but it is not their inherent possession" *(ibid.,* p. 148).

Exactly what are these theologians talking about? What scriptural evidence do they point to?

Let's take a brief look.

According to Scripture, the grave has no consciousness. "The dead know not any thing, neither have they any more a reward. . . . Also their love, and their hatred, and their envy, is now perished; neither have they any more a portion for ever in any thing that is done under the sun" (Eccl. 9:5, 6, KJV).

These verses alone sound a death knell to the idea that the dead live on after death, immediately receive a reward according to their deeds, and are thus reincarnated into another life-form based on their previous existence.

Note again the words "Neither have they any more a reward" and "neither have they any more a portion for ever in any thing that is done under the sun." Death is pretty much final, according to this biblical passage.

This understanding of death has its roots in the Creation story, which states that God "breathed into [Adam's] nostrils the breath of life; and man became a living soul" (Gen. 2:7, NKJV).

From that verse it is possible to adduce a formula:

living soul = breath of life + dead body

By using an algebraic-type formula, we can also deduce that the opposite formula is also accurate:

dead body = living soul – breath of life

Clearly that is a logical deduction, but can Scripture support it?

For all practical purposes, it appears that this same basic formula is found in Ecclesiastes 12:7: "Then shall the dust return to the earth as it was: and the spirit [Hebrew: breath] shall return unto God who gave it" (KJV).

And we find more to buttress this line of reasoning: "All go unto one place; all are of the dust, and all turn to dust again" (Eccl. 3:20, KJV). Interestingly, that verse appears in the context of comparing the death of human beings with the death of animals. The writer of Ecclesiastes indicates that *both* animals *and* humans encounter the same kind of death. Ecclesiastes 3:19-21 sees no difference between their fates.

Since the apostle Paul insists that only God has immortality (1 Tim. 6:16), we can infer that no human beings are immortal or have immortal souls. Death, then, is a sleep—an unconscious state, because death has no love or hate or jealousy or knowledge or working or planning (Eccl. 9:6, 10). "The living know that they will die, but the dead know nothing" (verse 5). Because death is like sleep, Christians have called their burial places cemeteries, a term that comes from a Greek word meaning sleeping chamber or bedroom.

So according to this understanding of Scripture, there is no existence preceding life and none after death—except at the resurrection of the dead, which takes place at the second coming of Jesus. The soul is not immortal, then, if this view is correct.

Clearly, Christians need not have any sympathy with the concept that the evils that befall us now are the results of what we did in a previous life, *if*—and that is a big "if"—they stick to the biblical evidence demonstrating that humans are psychosomatic unities and upon death sleep in the grave, awaiting an eschatological resurrection.

Such a biblical perspective repudiates the philosophy that lies behind the concept of reincarnation. Without immortal souls, people can hardly be reincarnated. So poor Bill Simpson was not suffering for something he did in a previous existence, because he never had a prior life.

Perhaps it might be wiser to point out to Bill and his fellow sufferers that despite the evils we must endure during our existence on Planet Earth, a future existence awaits us in which justice and mercy will ever prevail.

### WHEN GOD'S HEART BREAKS:

*"I have chosen you and have not rejected you. So do not fear, for I
am with you; do not be dismayed, for I am your God.
I will strengthen you and help you; I will uphold you
with my righteous right hand" (Isa. 41:9, 10).*

# CHAPTER FIVE

## Sarah—Grin and Bear It

Sarah Carter—we know her last name but not her first, so we'll give her a first name—was 8 years old. She and her mother—Marilyn Carter (age 35)—and her stepfather—John Medina (age 31)—lived with her grandmother in an apartment in New York City.

When she was 4 years old, little Sarah developed a healthy appetite, as growing children are likely to do. Sometimes it seemed as though she couldn't fill herself up. (Parents know all about that, and when I was growing up they frequently talked about a child with a hearty appetite having a "hollow leg.") And when there wasn't enough food on the table, little Sarah resorted to stealing some—to satisfy her hunger.

Clearly, such a voracious appetite needed to be curbed. So what did her parents do?

Did they make Sarah take Dexatrim? Or Ultra Slim Fast?

Did they enroll the child in Weight Watchers?

Did they feed her Lean Cuisine?

Did they make her exercise along with Jane Fonda on videotape?

Did they make her watch Susan Powter on television?

No. They had a better plan.

Marilyn and John decided to ration Sarah's meals—one every two weeks! That's right, two meals a month.

What does a starving girl do?

She fusses a lot.

Well, Marilyn and John had a solution for that also.

They'd handcuff Sarah—*upside down*—to the bathtub faucets and beat her with a hammer and pour scalding water over her and then use a scouring pad or sandpaper to scrape off her scalded skin.

One time when Mama was beating her daughter in the face—Sarah was now 8 years old—she split open Sarah's eyelid. Instead of dialing 9-1-1 or taking Sarah to the emergency room of the local hospital, Mama decided to give Sarah immediate first aid. She sewed the eyelid herself with a needle and thread.

For four long years the abuse continued. Finally, Sarah's 71-year-old grandmother could stand it no longer and told a friend, who in turn contacted the police.

Officer Virginia Grimm—a fitting name, don't you think?—reported that Sarah's "wrists were swollen, her stomach was swollen, there was obvious malnutrition." Officer Grimm added more details: "There were lacerations on her neck; it looked like her neck had been scraped by a cheese grater. She had hair missing where the mother had pulled it out in large clumps."

"There wasn't three inches of unscarred skin on her whole body," Officer Grimm concluded.

Little Sarah was rushed to Lincoln Hospital, where she was treated and listed in stable condition *(The Morning Herald,* Sept. 30, 1993, p. 1).

Fortunately for Sarah, she didn't lose her life despite the terrible cruelty perpetrated on her.

Suppose that you were the social worker who had to deal with the child. You had to take her aside and explain to her that what she had endured for all these years was not typical of what most children go through. That being tortured as she had been is not really part of the process of growing up.

Since you happen to be a devoutly religious social worker, you feel that a little spiritual encouragement might also help her. What should you tell her? Would you encourage her to keep a stiff upper lip despite all these bad things that happened to her?

Should Sarah take a stoical approach to life?

"Grin and bear it, Sarah," you exhort her.

What about such advice?

First, we need to realize that this is *not* an explanation for why bad things have happened. The stoical advice to grin and bear it has no possible explanatory power.

Instead, this counsel simply informs the sufferer—Sarah, in this instance—how he or she should behave under the circumstances.

And this leads us to the second point. If you yourself have not suffered as Sarah has, what makes you think that you have the right to advise her about the attitude she should have?

You are not the one starving.

You are not the one handcuffed to the tub.

You are not the one beaten with a hammer.

You are not the one scalded.

You are not the one who had the burns scraped with a scouring pad.

You are not the one who had an eyelid sewn shut with a regular sewing needle and cotton thread.

So why should you—or I, for that matter—feel qualified to tell Sarah what kind of attitude would be appropriate for her?

Third, I think that we should try to put ourselves in Sarah's place. How would we like it if we had to endure the cruelty she has suffered and then have someone tell us to grin and bear it? to keep a stiff upper lip?

A little empathy on our part would quickly show up the fallacy—no, the callousness—of this response to human misery.

I forget now the circumstances, but one day things were especially bad for me at work, and I was chafing under the situation. So that week I telephoned my parents. I remember explaining to my dad what had gone on. And he, usually a very sensitive person, responded to my tale of woe with some advice on how to relate to others.

But I hadn't told him about my difficulties so that he could give me some admonition. I didn't want counsel. All I wanted was a sympathetic ear. I only wanted to hear something such as "That's too bad, son. I'm sorry."

Similarly, Sarah doesn't need an insensitive response such as "Buck up, Sarah!"

Life is too full of too many tragic things that happen for us to be so heartless as to tell sufferers to keep a stiff upper lip.

Fourth, a little kindness in such situations can go a long way.

People like Sarah do not need lectures.

They do not need rebukes.

They do not need lessons.

Or discourses.

Or instructions.

In fact, they really do not need tutelage or explanations in any form.

What, then, do they need? They need our sympathy. our empathy. our encouragement. our understanding. our approval. They need our support.

Around 3:30 in the morning, Saturday, December 17, 1994, the persistent ringing of the phone finally penetrated the fog of sleep that enshrouded me. "Richard, this is Mother," and the voice broke. "Dad just died." Suddenly a wave of shock rolled in and replaced the fog of drowsiness. Dad. Dead! Gone.

As soon as I hung up the phone, I dialed United Airlines and booked tickets for the next available flight to Ontario, California. Then followed a shower, a quick meal, packing, and the 90-minute trip to the airport.

While waiting for my flight to board, I phoned my younger son, Ron. I knew that by now he'd be awake and up and around. "Ron, this is Dad."

"Yes, Dad."

"My dad just died."

Silence. Nothing. Was Ron still there? Had he hung up? No, there was no dial tone. I proceeded to explain the circumstances, but the boarding announcement interrupted. So I kissed my wife goodbye and handed the phone to her. She could finish the story while I sat in my cramped airline seat.

The more I have reflected on Ron's response, the more appropriate I realize it was. Not only did his silence reflect his own shock and sorrow, but it also complemented and reflected my own. Sometimes silence is more comforting and meaningful than any words we could possibly think of. Additionally, I see his silence as a human revelation of God's silence. So often in our grief and anguish we listen for a word from God, and all we hear is silence. We can interpret that silence as indicating God's lack of interest. On the other hand, it can mirror our own anguish. God's silence can reveal to us His own distress because of our suffering.

Let's not tell the Sarahs of our world to buck up, to keep a stiff upper lip, to grin and bear it.

That's sheer cruelty.

And it does no one any good. It hurts both the person to whom it is said and the person who says it.

It hardens hearts. Which is just the opposite of what God wants to do for us. He longs to give us hearts of flesh for our normal hearts of stone (Eze. 11:19; 36:26).

Perhaps it would be best to forget about giving Sarah advice and to let down our defenses and weep sympathetically with her. That may say more to her than any passel of words.

### WHEN GOD'S HEART BREAKS:
*"For I am the Lord, your God, who takes hold of*
*your right hand and says to you, Do not fear;*
*I will help you" (Isa. 41:13).*

# CHAPTER SIX

## Myra—It's Your Vocation

Myra Collins was a dedicated Christian mother with six lively but wonderful children: Tommy, Johnny, Sandra, Sharon, Susie, and Becky. All the children but Becky, as I recall, were classmates of mine in New London, Connecticut.

They lived out in the country, and it was always fun to go to their place and play. In the winter I skated (or tried to skate) on their pond. I wish I could have blamed my disastrous attempts on the bumpiness of the ice, but the truth is that because of my clumsiness and weak ankles I went through more gyrations than Olympic figure skaters.

One summer evening we spent a pleasant time following a waddling skunk around their property! Fortunately, we had enough sense to stay our distance.

Then another December rolled around, and everyone was getting ready for Christmas. Suddenly Myra took ill and began feeling pretty terrible. A well-meaning neighbor, who thrived on natural remedies, gave her some cayenne pepper pills (which were supposed to cure just about anything), but Myra didn't get any better.

Why was the flu holding on so long?

Finally, on Christmas Eve, Myra asked her husband, Tom, to contact the doctor. The physician immediately knew what Myra's problem was—polio, for this was the 1950s, and polio was, unfortunately, not infrequent in that part of Connecticut.

The tiny local hospital didn't do a very good job in caring

for Myra, who was now in an iron lung. (You may recall that iron lungs were body-length canisters in which patients were placed, with their head protruding. The machine breathed for the patients.)

For instance, Myra had espoused a vegetarian diet, and when a harried nurse tried to feed her some meat, Myra refused to eat it. The nurse didn't know Myra very well, or she would have known that she was a kind, gentle, patient woman. But the nurse assumed that Myra was merely trying to be stubborn. Finally, in a pique of anger, the nurse picked up Myra's glass of ice water and flung it into her face!

Since there wasn't a nearby hospital with adequate facilities for a polio victim, the attending physician decided that he needed to transfer Myra to a larger facility. In fact, he felt that it would be best if she moved to a hospital in Boston. There she could receive the care that was so critical.

So a small caravan formed to drive her to Boston, Massachusetts. Orderlies rolled Myra's iron lung into a rental truck equipped with an electric generator to keep the life-sustaining machine in operation. An ambulance carrying other supplies followed it. Tom and other family members rode in a car behind the ambulance. My dad, mother, and I followed the Collins family. And a bevy of cops headed the procession and took up the rear.

With police sirens screaming in front and behind, we roared off from New London, Connecticut, to Boston, Massachusetts. I was only about 13 or 14, I guess, and never had experienced such an exciting ride! We whizzed through stoplights and exceeded the speed limit as we raced down the highway toward Boston.

When U.S. 1 crossed into Rhode Island, a new set of state troopers waited for us. The Connecticut state police pulled to the side of the road, and the Rhode Island state police zoomed ahead and behind. Somewhere in Rhode Island, as I recall, one of the motorcycle cops almost got wiped out by a car that wasn't willing to yield the right-of-way. At the Massachusetts state line the same changing of the guard took place. I could hardly contain myself because of the thrill of it all.

At one point en route the engine in the rental truck sputtered, and the truck stalled. It coasted to the side of the highway. Now what to do? With the engine not running, it was impossible to lower the truck's power tailgate in order to get to Myra. If the engine remained persistent in its balkiness, the gasoline-driven electric generator that powered the iron lung would run out of fuel, leaving Myra imprisoned inside the cargo area of the truck to suffocate to death. Fortunately, a little mechanical tweaking got the truck's engine purring once more.

Finally we unloaded Myra at the hospital in Boston, where she got proper treatment. The staff at this large hospital quickly fell in love with her and her gentle disposition and gave her meticulous care.

For a few weeks her daughter Sharon came to live at my home. That was something new to me, because I'm an only child. As I look back on it now, I realize that I found it difficult to share my home and my parents and my toys with someone else. I fear that I frequently treated the girl as an intruder. And when I helped brush her hair at night before she went to bed or in the morning when she got up, I wasn't as gentle as I should have been. Sharon would screw up her face and whimper. But really, she was an exemplary child, despite my callousness.

After intensive treatment and rehabilitation of sorts, Myra graduated to a portable respirator. At that point she was ready to return home, and ultimately she went from the respirator to a rocking bed. Its constant seesaw motion somehow helped her breathe. At home her children waited on her hand and foot—feeding her, giving her liquids to drink, combing her hair, bathing her, manicuring her nails, helping her eliminate bodily wastes.

I remember praying for Myra every morning and every night, asking God to heal her. And sometimes at night as I thought about Myra while I lay in bed, I got the distinct inkling that I should go to her side, take her by the hand, and tell her to get up and walk! I'm not sure exactly why that notion came to me, but I mentioned it to my mother, who told Myra. Myra replied, "Next time Richard has that feeling, bring him by."

Several years elapsed before Myra succumbed, maybe to a

cold or the flu or pneumonia, leaving six children motherless. It was a sad funeral.

Alas, all the prayers for Myra's healing had come to naught.

Suppose, for a few minutes, that you had known Myra. What would you have told her during her ordeal? Would you have suggested, as some Christians do, that suffering was her vocation?

The word "vocation" comes from a Latin word that means "calling." It describes a person's lifework. But the word has connotations that lift it above regular labor or toil. It has something of prestige about it. That's because

(1) vocations are careers that we generally select or choose, although there may be some kind of ancillary motive that prompts us to make the choice and

(2) vocations are also something that we normally train for—when you have a vocation you must have certain qualifications and

(3) vocations generally are service-oriented—they provide help for others and

(4) vocations usually involve a certain amount of professionalism—one behaves in a competent manner that meets certain expectations.

But is suffering from polio a vocation? Is contracting bone cancer a vocation? Is being a quadriplegic a vocation?

Let's look at those criteria for a vocation again, and see if they apply to someone who is suffering, as Myra was and others do.

1. Is going blind, for example, something that we select or choose?

Throughout the years I've made the acquaintance of several blind people. I remember Raymond, who was born blind. His eyes were clearly sightless and looked terribly strange as they darted about almost randomly.

Sarah was probably in her late 40s or 50s and could read braille with great skill. I recall when Mother had her over to our place for a meal. Sarah "looked" around the kitchen and said, "I just love your color scheme—blue and yellow." Mother was flabbergasted, because she'd had Dad paint the walls yellow and had made yellow-and-blue curtains!

Bob worked in the same office complex as I, and he maneuvered from office to office with great freedom of movement despite his blindness. I needed only to say "Hi, Bob," and he immediately called me by name. Shortly after he retired he gained local fame by diving into a swimming pool and saving the life of a drowning person.

And then, of course, there was world-famous Helen Keller, who was not only blind but also deaf. We often quote her words because of her deep insights and pithy way of putting things. But I don't recall that she ever said, "Yes, I chose to become blind and deaf because it was something I always wanted." Nor did Raymond or Sarah or Bob.

2. How does one train to be born with muscular dystrophy or cerebral palsy? And is there a school that teaches how to prepare oneself to be autistic?

Billy was born with muscular dystrophy and for all practical purposes had no overt control over his muscles. Saliva constantly drooled from his mouth. It was difficult to look at him, and as a child I felt profoundly uncomfortable in his presence.

Linda was about 4 years old and had cerebral palsy. She was spastic, and her arms would flail about and her head jerk. Her speech was so jumbled that most of the time only her parents could understand what she was saying. Yet her mind was sharp, imprisoned in a body that simply couldn't function well.

Charlie was autistic. You might talk to him, but he generally behaved as if he were the only person in all the world. His parents went through emotional hell for years as they heard authorities speak about aloof and cold parents triggering autism. They knew that they weren't that way, and they had several other children without disabilities, but why had Charlie withdrawn into himself and blocked out the rest of the world?

Yet Billy, Linda, and Charlie hadn't gone to school so that they could learn to have muscular dystrophy or cerebral palsy or autism. In fact, instead of having trained so that they could get these impairments, they needed training to help them cope.

Their ailments may have plagued them throughout life, but they were hardly vocations.

3. When Aunt Eleanor came down with multiple sclerosis, was that service-oriented? Did she suddenly become more of a help to herself, to her family, to her community? Hardly.

She had been working for the Aetna Insurance Company when she began to fall, sometimes for no apparent reason. And occasionally she'd drop something and wonder why. As the symptoms became more obvious, she sought out a physician. The diagnosis was devastating—multiple sclerosis. Soon she had to quit work.

Before long, Aunt Eleanor couldn't walk easily. Her legs somehow didn't want to obey what her brain was telling them to do. Her hands became the same way—impervious to her will. Then her eyesight became abnormal. And her hearing became so sensitive that almost any noise sent stabbing pain through her head.

For a while Aunt Eleanor got around using a walker, shuffling from one room to another. The doctor fitted her with special braces on her arms and hands. Finally she was confined to bed. The last time I saw her before she died, Aunt Eleanor looked like a skeleton with skin drawn about it. She was totally bedfast and had to be waited on constantly. Although she could barely see, she knew I was there and tried to speak a few words.

On one occasion Aunt Eleanor told her sister that when she felt at her worst, she'd spend hours in prayer, petitioning God for her children, her grandson, her husband, her brothers, her sisters, her nephews, her nieces, her great-nephews and great-nieces. She'd picture each one in her mind and then ask God's richest blessings upon them.

But for all practical purposes, as we often say, Aunt Eleanor was not fitted for a life of service, because of her multiple sclerosis. She was no longer able to work, to clean house, to cook, to go to church, to baby-sit her grandson, to visit the sick, to attend funerals—except her own.

4. When William Howard contracted Alzheimer's disease, did his behavior exhibit professionalism? Was his mindlessness when he stuffed a towel into the toilet bowl and flushed the toi-

let, causing water to cascade down the stairs into the living room, competent behavior?

Mr. Howard had a noble face and lovely white hair. A handsome man, he looked pretty much like a banker or a doctor or a professor. But as I sat in his living room and chatted with his wife, he slumped immobile in an overstuffed chair. Occasionally he would make some inane comment, and his wife would solicitously address him. But William Howard was totally out of it. He didn't know who I was, and he didn't know who his wife was. In fact, he didn't even know who he was.

He might have looked like a professional of some sort, but Alzheimer's didn't make him behave competently. In his younger days he had been quite adept, but not now.

"Oh, but wait!" you might say. "The concept of being 'called' to suffer is biblical. Haven't you read 1 Peter 2:21? It says: 'For even hereunto were ye called: because Christ also suffered for us, leaving us an example, that ye should follow his steps'" (KJV).

It is true, of course, that this passage is in the Bible, and I have no argument with it. At first glance several terms in the passage catch our attention: "called," "suffered," "example," and "should follow." One is therefore tempted to conclude that suffering is the calling of Christians, because Jesus is their example, and He suffered. In fact, one might then switch terms and arrive at: Polio is the vocation of Myra, because Jesus is her role model, and He suffered.

I do not, however, think that 1 Peter 2:21 delivers a death blow to the line of argumentation I have pursued in this chapter. Why? Because a careful reading of the passage puts us on another track. When we interpret a Bible verse we need to ask such questions as: What is the immediate context of the passage? To whom is the verse addressed? And what does the language denote?

So let's take a closer look at 1 Peter 2:21.

*What is the immediate context of this verse?* Verse 21 is part of a paragraph that begins with verse 18 and ends with verse 25. (Some may want to divide the paragraph differently.) And this paragraph is part of a larger portion in which Peter admonishes various categories of people, which begins with verse 1 and ends with chapter 4, verse 19. More about this later.

*To whom is the verse addressed?* Peter is talking to Christians— Gentile Christians, to be exact (verses 9, 10). He is also addressing various subcategories of Christians: slaves (verse 18), wives (1 Peter 3:1), husbands (verse 7), and all Gentile Christians (verse 8). The particular people in mind in 1 Peter 2:21 are slaves. They are to be model servants so that if they indeed suffer, it is not for their misdeeds but because they are exemplary and their masters are treating them wrongfully (verses 18, 19).

*And what does the language denote?* Yes, the word "suffer" is used. But what kind of suffering does Peter have in mind here? Huntington's disease? Does he mean the loss of a house in a flood? Is he referring to a 3-year-old squished under the tires of a hit-and-run drunk driver?

No. Peter is talking about having one's good behavior punished, not bad behavior. Here are some of his terms of reference: you are called evildoers, but your good works are seen and glorify God (verse 12); your well-doing will silence foolish men (verse 15); your freedom is not a cloak for malicious behavior (verse 16); in honoring your own conscience you may endure grief and suffer wrongfully (verse 19); you may suffer for doing well (verse 20); Christ never did anything wrong, nevertheless He suffered (verses 21, 22); you may suffer for righteousness' sake (1 Peter 3:14); people who accuse you of doing evil will be ashamed because of your goodness (verse 16); it is better to suffer for doing good than for doing evil (verse 17); Christ suffered for sins—not His, but the just for the unjust (verse 18); people will speak evil of you (1 Peter 4:4); a fiery trial will try you (verse 12); you will be reproached for Christ's name (verse 14); and don't suffer as a murderer or thief or evildoer (verse 15).

Each instance is not speaking of random or gratuitous suffering, but persecution. Persecution, as we all know, is being punished (hence, suffering) unjustly for either being good or doing good.

And that is precisely the kind of suffering that Jesus endured, according to Peter. Jesus was sinless, yet He suffered. What was His suffering? Epilepsy? Muscular dystrophy? No. His suffering was because of His exemplary life (1 Peter 2:21-24).

So the "calling" to which Peter refers is simply a vocation of persecution. And the early Christians were no strangers to persecution. So this passage is best understood as referring to persecution and hence is not germane to the subject of random disaster, disease, and death. The same applies to similar passages, such as Matthew 5:11; Romans 5:3; 2 Corinthians 1:3-7; 4:8-18; Philippians 1:12-14, 19; Hebrews 10:34; James 1:2; 1 Peter 1:6, 7; 3:17; 4:13, 14; and 4:19.

The first Christians were no strangers to persecution, and it didn't surprise them. They remembered that in the Sermon on the Mount Jesus had predicted that people would revile His followers and accuse them falsely of all sorts of things (Matt. 5:11). But the members of His kingdom could consider themselves blessed when so persecuted (verses 10, 11). In fact, they could even rejoice, because heaven would greatly reward them for their faithfulness (verse 12).

John 15:20 echoes Peter's instruction in 1 Peter 2:21-24. Jesus told His followers that just as He had been persecuted, so they would be. "The servant," He said, "is not greater than his lord" (KJV).

Paul reminded the Christians in Corinth that the apostles suffered persecution, but painful though it may be, the apostle regarded it as light and momentary when contrasted with the "eternal weight of glory" awaiting them (2 Cor. 4:17, KJV).

The reasons behind persecution are obvious. Those persecuted know that they are suffering for a cause—for the right. They never had to ask why this was happening, because they knew why. It was their privilege to witness—even in death—to their faith in Jesus. As a result, they could rejoice—not because they relished the pain but because they knew God had called them to this testimony.

Throughout history Christians (as well as faithful adherents to other religions) have endured persecution. They regard it as their vocation. But for Myra and countless others disaster, disease, and death appear to have little meaning. Terribly random, it strikes believer and unbeliever alike.

Should we tell victims that suffering is their vocation? No. It's more like a cruel joke to equate their pain with their profession.

It is true, of course, that some people manage to find the inner resources to suffer bravely and nobly. Aunt Vera, severely crippled with rheumatoid arthritis, somehow found it within her to remain sweet and cheery—despite the constant agony in practically every joint of her body. She's been dead for many years now, but I can still recall her knobby knuckles and contorted feet.

But such behavior in the face of suffering, admirable as it is, hardly means that those afflicted should regard suffering as a vocation. Indeed, I see no reason in all the world why anyone should ever view their suffering as a vocation.

There's nothing inherently noble in hurting.

There's nothing especially admirable in pain.

There's nothing particularly virtuous in torment.

So let's not try to paste a smiley face on disaster, disease, and death. Such a facade helps no one.

Surely it would be better to tell the Myras of the world that as terrible and appalling as their suffering may be, God still looks on them with love and sympathy and longs for the time when they will enjoy unending health. Indeed, He is working toward that end this very moment.

### WHEN GOD'S HEART BREAKS:
*"For a long time I have kept silent, I have been quiet and held myself back. But now, like a woman in childbirth, I cry out, I gasp and pant" (Isa. 42:14).*

# CHAPTER SEVEN

## Oklahoma City— You're Expendable

Nine a.m. April 19, 1995. The 450,000 people of Oklahoma City—almost a world away from New York City and Los Angeles, with their burgeoning crime—were gearing up for another sunny day and business as usual.

At the Alfred P. Murrah Federal Building civil servants were pretty much ready for another hectic day. Executives already were pressing phone handsets against their ears. Secretaries were opening and shutting file drawers. Clients were sitting in waiting areas, bored or tapping their fingers nervously on countertops. Twenty-four babies and toddlers were already sucking on bottles or playing with blocks and balls and dolls. Some were fussy; others giggled in pleasure.

9:01. Ho-hum. Another day. Another typical Wednesday.

9:02. *Kaboom!*

A rental truck parked outside the edifice violently exploded. Cars parked across the street did flips, crumpled, then burst into flames. Within a four-block radius, windows shattered and walls cracked. Twenty-five miles distant people heard the noise—and thought an earthquake had struck.

Eight seconds later near the point of the explosion stretched a crater 20 feet wide and eight feet deep. The front part of the Alfred P. Murrah building had crumbled into a mass of shattered glass, twisted steel, and fragmented concrete 27 feet deep.

You saw the photos. You watched the news. You were riveted along with the rest of America as the drama unfolded in newspapers, weekly magazines, radiobroadcasts, and television newscasts.

What caused the explosion? About a ton of fertilizer mixed with fuel oil and aluminum powder until it was the consistency of oatmeal and then dumped into 20 to 22 blue plastic 55-gallon drums that were later stuffed into the rented truck.

Why? Prosecutors busied themselves trying to unravel motives. We did hear, however, a lot about militia groups and disgruntled Americans and possible retaliation for the government's assault on the Branch Davidian headquarters in Waco, Texas.

How many lives had been snuffed out during the eight-second explosion? It would take days for the final tally. On Thursday, May 4, we knew. One hundred sixty-eight dead. Nineteen of them babies!

Imagine that you're one of the pastors and chaplains who rushed to the scene after hearing about the shocking tragedy. Now you're at the hospital or at one of the emergency centers the authorities quickly set up. Grief-stricken mothers and devastated fathers and dazed husbands and hurting wives gaze in shock and horror at you. They hunger for your explanation.

And what do you say?

Maybe you should share with these heartsick men and women the interesting explanation proposed by Pastor Harvy Wilcox, a personal friend of mine.

I first became acquainted with him when I was a child in Connecticut. He was a church leader in the area, and on occasion my parents invited him to our home for a meal. The two of us hit it off pretty well. I held him in something of awe, and he regarded me as a "good boy."

Later, when I was in my senior year at college, it fell my lot to work for the organization he headed as president. It was at this same time, just prior to graduation, that I had to face Pastor Wilcox in his large office and ask for a few days off so that I could go on a honeymoon with my soon-to-be wife. What would he say? I stood before him nervously, shaking inside.

"Richard," he replied, "you should have asked for a year off, because that's what the Old Testament allows for newly married men. They don't have to work for a whole year." Then as a smile crossed his face, he told me that he was pleased I was getting married and of course I could have a few days off.

But exactly what words of comfort did Pastor Wilcox have for sufferers? "We may be expendable in the successful execution of God's cosmic plan," he suggested. "The mature Christian is eventually able to say: 'If God sees that I am expendable, so be it.'"

So perhaps you should tell the grieving mommies and daddies of Oklahoma City that their babies were expendable in God's great plan. As a consoling chaplain maybe you should inform the sobbing husbands and wives that their spouses were expendable as God proved a point to humanity and the rest of the universe.

Would they find consolation in knowing that their nearest and dearest were expendable? How would you feel if someone passed that choice bit of information along to you? Would it soothe your breaking heart? Would it charge your life with new meaning?

This stern approach to suffering basically tells us that life is God's game of chess and that God is the great chess master, playing chess with the devil. The pieces on the board are human beings, and God and Satan challenge each other in the cosmic game of life. Who will win? The devil? God? What will happen to the pieces on the board of life?

Now, chess is a fascinating game first played in Asia, perhaps originating in India. In fact, its name comes from the Iranian word for king—*shah*. You undoubtedly know that it is played on a board of 64 squares that alternate between dark and light colors. On the board each of the two players places 16 men—eight pawns, two rooks or castles, two knights, two bishops, one queen, and one king. Each of the pieces can move according to certain rules. Some can shift only one space in a specific direction, while others may move several places. Some can go only diagonally, some only in an L-shape, and others straight back and forth or from left to right and vice versa.

The object of the game is to make the opposing king surrender—to checkmate him. In order to win the game, the victor *of necessity* is going to lose some pieces in the process of waging the game. In short, the chess pieces are expendable. As long as you get the other king checkmated, it really does not matter how many pawns or knights or bishops or rooks you lose.

According to the concept that those of us who suffer are expendable for God's sake, God is the grand chess master. He has set up His pieces on the board—the pawns, the rooks, knights, bishops, queen, and king. Almost all these are expendable while God plays the game to protect the king—Himself, or His reputation. (The analogy breaks down here a bit because God suddenly becomes not only the skilled chess master but also one of the pieces on the board—the king.)

Since God is the grand chess master and Satan has lesser skill, it is pretty much a foregone conclusion that God will win the game. But in order to win, it is inevitable that He will have to sacrifice some of His pieces. Perhaps many pawns. Maybe both rooks or both knights or both bishops. He might even have to sacrifice the queen. They are expendable, but by being expendable they enable God to win the cosmic chess game in which all of us are involved.

❤ ❤ ❤

This explanation of suffering is pretty much a variation on the theme of the great controversy between God and Satan, the struggle between good and evil. So the comments in the chapter dealing with that topic in *When God Sheds Tears* are just as appropriate here. The chief difference, it seems to me, is that the chess analogy is a bit more whimsical. And to state that each of us is expendable is simply a bit more blatant. But the same dynamics are involved. God is out to make His case. As the grand chess master of the universe, He will win the game. We are simply pawns for Him to do with in any way that He sees fit so that we can enable Him to checkmate the devil.

Alas, however, such a vision of life tends to dehumanize each of us. According to such a view, none of us has any inherent value as a human being. Our worth is in not *who* we are but in *what* we can do—what we can do for God so that He can checkmate Satan, making him, in chess terminology, "resign."

This emphasis that we are expendable like pieces in chess reminds me of something the great philosopher Immanuel Kant once said. Kant insisted that we must never treat human beings only as means to an end but as ends in and of themselves.

The more one reflects on this advice, the more one recognizes its wisdom. To regard other people as means to an end, argued Kant, is immoral. To do so "thingifies" them. It detracts from—no, it destroys—their humanity. Human beings are not things—not pawns—on a cosmic chessboard.

Rather, human beings are living creatures with minds and feelings. God created us in His image. And so our fellow human beings are worthy of being treated as persons. We should not, therefore, treat others as means to an end. Instead, we should honor their dignity, respect the image of God that they bear, and so regard them as ends in themselves.

That each of us bears the image of God in our very nature constitutes the basis of a special ethic. Because others bear the divine image, when I see them I should also view behind their human nature God Himself. It is not that each person is inherently divine. That is an aspect of Eastern mysticism. The biblical doctrine of humans having been created in God's image emphasizes rather our own creatureliness, but it also helps us see beyond our earthiness to God Himself.

You are not God, and I am not God. But somehow in our existence we can point to God, our Creator. So when I see you, someone bearing the Creator's image, I should treat you with deference similar to that with which I would approach God Himself. And when you see me, you should see more than a poor human creature but beyond to God Himself, whose image I bear. Therefore you should treat me with the respect that you'd show toward God. This is an ethic based on mutual respect and deference because we can see beyond mere externals to something of far more worth than mere creatureliness.

When we treat others with mutual esteem, we will not depersonalize them. To do this means that they are not expendable or extraneous. People are important and useful in and of themselves. As theologian Martin Buber used to argue, we can—and should—relate to each other as an "I" to a "thou" rather than as an "I" to an "it." This perspective emphasizes relationship. We also must have a relationship with God based on "I-thou" rather than "I-it."

We humans do not gain our significance simply because we stand ready to be used in any way God deems necessary to save face. To suggest that we are all expendable, it seems to me, is too stern a judgment. And to propose that we are all dispensable is too severe a doctrine.

Of course, some cultures have regarded individuals as expendable. Kamikaze pilots went on suicide missions. So did the Viet Cong. So do Muslim suicide bombers. Those on suicide missions know from the outset that they'll be killed. They and others truly regard themselves as expendable. Such a "commitment" most of us would regard as fanaticism, because generally in warfare we know that some soldiers will never return, but we don't send them off with the certainty that they will be the specific persons killed. Instead we hope they won't be the random casualties of war.

Such dedication, especially in light of the possibility of death, is admirable. Committed people are considered valuable assets. On the other hand, *Webster's Collegiate Dictionary* defines the adjective "expendable" as that which is "more economically replaced than rescued, salvaged, or protected." That which is expendable gets used up because it generally lacks value.

It is this connotation to the word "expendable" to which I object. The term implies lack of value. And I don't for a moment believe that our heavenly Father regards any one of His children as having little or no worth. The Christian understanding is that God regards each of us as so important that Jesus would have died on Calvary even if there had been only one sinner in all the world.

The idea that Christians are expendable founders on the biblical picture of a God whose very nature is love. It collapses on God's attributes of holiness, righteousness, justice, and fairness.

Perhaps it would be more appropriate to point to our heavenly Father, who notices when a sparrow dies, and to Jesus, who would have gone to the cross for even one person.

## WHEN GOD'S HEART BREAKS:
*"Even to your old age and gray hairs I am he, I am he who will sustain you. I have made you and I will carry you; I will sustain you and I will rescue you"* (Isa. 46:4).

# CHAPTER EIGHT

## Sunshine and Rain

We were about halfway through a seminar based on my book *When God Sheds Tears* when Ed raised an important question based on two Bible passages. "Richard," he asked, "what about the psalmist's assurance: 'I was young and now I am old, yet I have never seen the righteous forsaken or their children begging bread' [Ps. 37:25]? And what about God's promise through Malachi that if we tithe, He will open heaven's windows and pour out more blessing than we can possibly accept and will 'rebuke the devourer' for us [Mal. 3:10, 11, KJV]?"

Ed wasn't so much challenging as he was seeking. How *do* we understand these and other similar passages of Scripture? The issue becomes singularly poignant in light of the evidence.

First, consider the matter of the righteous never begging bread. The past half century has seen some sad statistics. From 1941 to 1944 more than 1 million persons died from starvation during the military siege of Leningrad. During 1943 some 50,000 starved in Rwanda-Urundi. In 1943 and 1944 India lost 1.5 million persons to a famine confined to the Bengal province alone.

Nigeria and Biafra made the news during 1967 to 1969, when 1.5 million persons died from starvation. From 1968 to 1974 in the Sahel, which has frequent droughts, 500,000 died during a prolonged famine. Within the confines of 1971 to 1973, 1.5 million starved to death in Ethiopia.

In Kampuchea (formerly Cambodia) from 1975 to 1979, 1 million succumbed during famine conditions. Again in 1983 to

1985 Sahel suffered another major drought, endangering 22 million people. In 1992, 250,000 men and women, boys and girls throughout the world, died from starvation.

What are we to make of such mind-boggling numbers? Were none of these victims Christians? none righteous? none a child of God? Clearly, it is not factual to assume that. So was the psalmist naive?

And second, what about Malachi's glowing promise of sure deliverance for tithe-payers? LaVerne and Eunice told me about her uncle, a grain farmer in Saskatchewan, Canada. Because he was a devout Christian who scrupulously tithed his income, it was exceedingly traumatic for him when a hailstorm bypassed the fields of neighboring farmers, who never tithed, and singled out his acreage, wiping out the entire crop (and a year's earnings). No "rebuke" for the "devourer" in his case.

Perhaps you're aware of similar circumstances.

Since at the time Ed raised the issue I was in the early stages of researching this chapter, I replied, "You've raised an important point, Ed, and I'm in the process of working on the issue. We all know of instances that fly in the face of these biblical passages. So how do we relate? That's what I'm studying."

This chapter and the two that follow present the fruit of my study. You may not find them very satisfying, and that's OK.

In fact, you may heartily disagree with the conclusions formed from the discussion in these chapters. That would not be surprising, but please be charitable with me—care to think the very best.

These chapters may also have an impact on your view of inspiration, because a popular conception of revelation and inspiration tends to unravel in the face of the evidence I will present. Remember, however, that this does not mean Scripture is not inspired. It is. But sometimes our understanding of inspiration needs revising.

Finally, this material does not make easy reading, and if your interest wanes within the first page or two, that's OK. Skip these three chapters and read the rest of the book, which tends to be less technical. But if you're intellectually adventurous, you might find what is here presented stimulating—and perhaps even insightful.

So here goes.

If you were to switch on your TV this evening and the local meteorologist reported, "We'll be blessed with good weather tomorrow, folks," what would you expect the weather to be like on the following day? Would you envision sunshine, or would you anticipate rain? If you live almost anywhere in the United States, you'd look forward to sunny skies. Right? And you just might schedule a picnic.

But suppose you lived in Palestine, especially in ancient times. If someone forecasted good weather, what would you expect? The preponderance of biblical evidence suggests that you would envision showers. That's right, rain! Exactly the opposite of what Americans would expect.

Why the difference? Because the United States is considered a temperate zone and Palestine is a subtropical zone, the climates of the two locations differ considerably. Therefore climate is one of two reasons that people in Hagerstown, Maryland, where I live, and those in Jerusalem of old assess what is "good" weather so differently.

The second reason for the difference in what the two areas would consider as "good" weather is that biblical Palestine was an agricultural society, whereas the society in many (if not most) parts of twentieth-century United States is more industrial than agricultural.

"Palestine was primarily an agricultural country. . . .

"The farmers' main concern was the lack of sufficient and stable water supply" (John J. Rousseau and Rami Arav, *Jesus and His World*, p. 8).

"Rain was life itself; to control the rain was to control life" (John Dominic Crossan, *The Historical Jesus*, p. 140).

Now we can blend some hard data.

Palestine—modern as well as biblical—has only two seasons, and they are very distinct. They are the dry season and the wet season.

The *dry season* lasts from about the first of May to the end of September or even mid-October. Of these five months, three to four of them are completely rainless. During this time of the year the skies are generally sunny and cloudless. Only 25 percent of the time during the dry season do clouds scuttle across the Palestinian sky, but typically there are no totally cloudy days.

High temperatures average around 72° F in May, 76° F in June, 77° F in July, 78° F in August, and 76° F in September. Seldom does it get hotter than 90° F, although Jerusalem has had a record high of 112° F. (Jericho, which is considerably lower in altitude than Jerusalem—in fact, well below sea level—frequently has temperatures hovering around 100° F. Its highest temperature reached 120° F!)

During this dry season nearly all vegetation withers and enters a dormant stage. The whole area looks like a desert, and the ground is parched and cracked and rock hard. "Those who have never been in Palestine in the rainy season, and who see the country for the first time at the end of the summer [the dry season], cannot believe that the land produces anything at all" *(The SDA Bible Dictionary,* p. 831).

The *wet season* begins around mid-October with what the Bible calls the "early" or "former" rain and ends in March with what Scripture terms the "latter" rain. During the four months of November, December, January, and February, Palestine gets 70 to 75 percent of its rain.

One way of measuring rain is by using what meteorologists call the "rain day." A rain day is a 24-hour period during which at least .1 millimeter of rain falls. Jerusalem has around 50 to 52 "rain days" each year. (By contrast, London has more than 300 "rain days" annually.)

Another way of measuring rain, of course, is in inches. Jerusalem usually averages between 19 to 25 inches of rain yearly, and Galilee gets about 45 inches annually. (As a point of comparison, Maryland gets about 40 to 44 inches of rain each year.)

Precipitation—Yearly Average for Selected Cities

| Place | Inches | Place | Inches |
|---|---|---|---|
| **United States** | | South Carolina, Charleston | 51.53 |
| Alabama, Mobile | 63.96 | South Dakota, Rapid City | 16.64 |
| Alaska, Anchorage | 15.91 | Tennessee, Nashville | 47.30 |
| Arizona, Phoenix | 07.66 | Texas, Houston | 46.07 |
| Arkansas, Little Rock | 72.10 | Utah, Salt Lake City | 16.18 |
| California, Death Valley | 01.80 | Vermont, Burlington | 34.47 |
| California, Los Angeles | 14.77 | Virginia, Richmond | 43.16 |
| Colorado, Denver | 15.40 | Washington, Seattle | 37.19 |
| Connecticut, Hartford | 44.14 | Wisconsin, Milwaukee | 32.93 |
| Delaware, Wilimington | 40.84 | Wyoming, Lander | 13.01 |
| District of Columbia | 38.63 | **Algeria**, Algiers | 30.00 |
| Florida, Miami | 55.91 | **Brazil**, São Paulo | 57.30 |
| Georgia, Atlanta | 50.77 | **Canada**, Montreal | 40.80 |
| Hawaii, Honolulu | 22.02 | **Chile**, Arica | 00.02 |
| Hawaii, Mt. Waialeale | 472.00 | **China**, Shanghai | 45.00 |
| Idaho, Boise | 12.11 | **Denmark**, Copenhagen | 23.30 |
| Illinois, Chicago | 35.82 | **Egypt**, Cairo | 01.10 |
| Indiana, Indianapolis | 39.94 | **England**, London | 22.90 |
| Iowa, Des Moines | 33.12 | **Ethiopia**, Addis Ababa | 48.70 |
| Kentucky, Louisville | 44.39 | **France**, Paris | 22.30 |
| Louisiana, New Orleans | 61.88 | **Germany**, Berlin | 23.10 |
| Maine, Portland | 44.34 | **Greece**, Athens | 15.80 |
| Maryland, Baltimore | 40.76 | **India**, Bombay | 71.20 |
| Massachusetts, Boston | 41.51 | **Iran**, Tehran | 09.70 |
| Michigan, Detroit | 32.62 | **Ireland**, Dublin | 29.70 |
| Minnesota, Minneapolis /St. Paul | 28.32 | | |
| Mississippi, Jackson | 55.37 | **Israel**, Jerusalem | 19.70 |
| Missouri, St. Louis | 37.51 | **Italy**, Rome | 29.50 |
| Montana, Helena | 11.60 | **Japan**, Tokyo | 61.60 |
| Nebraska, Omaha | 29.86 | **Lebanon**, Beirut | 35.10 |
| Nevada, Reno | 07.53 | **Libya**, Tripoli | 15.10 |
| New Jersey, Atlantic City | 40.29 | **Netherlands**, Amsterdam | 25.60 |
| New Mexico, Albuquerque | 08.88 | **New Zealand**, Auckland | 49.10 |
| New York, New York City | 42.12 | **Poland**, Warsaw | 22.00 |
| North Carolina, Raleigh | 41.43 | **Russia**, Moscow | 24.80 |
| North Dakota, Bismarck | 15.47 | **Spain**, Madrid | 16.50 |
| Ohio, Cleveland | 36.63 | **Switzerland**, Geneva | 33.90 |
| Oregon, Portland | 36.30 | **Syria**, Damascus | 08.60 |
| Pennsylvania, Philadelphia | 41.41 | **Thailand**, Bangkok | 57.80 |
| Rhode Island, Providence | 45.53 | **Turkey**, Istanbul | 31.50 |

So it is not so much the *amount* of rain that is critical as it is the *number* of "rain days" and the *timing* of the rain. In Maryland precipitation is pretty much scattered throughout the year, but in Palestine that is not the case. The early rain is terribly important because it softens the dry, hard soil, thus making it plowable. The timing of the latter rain is also vital, because it gives the crops the last shot of moisture needed to push them to maturation. But if it comes too late, it can destroy the very grain that it is supposed to benefit. Palestine, unlike Egypt and Mesopotamia, does not have large permanently flowing rivers to use for irrigation.

"Especially in Palestine, timing, quantity, and quality of rain must work together in delicate harmony. Hours of heavy rain in September, for example, after months of aridity, could wash away topsoil completely. Not too much and not too little; not too soon and not too late" *(The Historical Jesus,* p. 140). Rainfall can also be spotty. One area might receive a torrential downpour while the land only a few miles away remains dry.

So because Palestine has a subtropical climate with only two seasons and because in Bible times Palestine was basically an agrarian culture, both the amount and timing of rain were absolutely critical. If the land received no rain or if it came at the wrong times, entire crops could fail and the people would go hungry. Ancient populations were always only one harvest away from starvation. They had no way to bring in surplus food from other more favored areas.

No wonder, then, that people in Bible times considered "good" weather rainy weather!

With this information in mind, we can now turn to the scriptural evidence itself. And we will begin with Deuteronomy, because at this point we're concerned with what biblical scholars call Deuteronomistic theology.

*"If you faithfully obey* the commands I am giving you today . . . *then I will send rain* on your land in its season, both autumn [early] and spring [latter] rains. . . . And you will eat and be sat-

isfied. *Be careful,* or you will be enticed to turn away and worship other gods and bow down to them. Then the Lord's anger will burn against you, and he will shut the heavens so that *it will not rain,* . . . and you will soon perish from the good land the Lord is giving you" (Deut. 11:13-17).

God draws the contrast in stark terms. Through Moses He warns His people that if they are "good," they will enjoy "good" weather—the early and latter rains. However, if they are "bad," they will suffer under "bad" weather—always sunny days. Famine will ensue, and they'll starve to death.

Later in Deuteronomy Moses speaks of the same blessing from God: "The Lord will open the heavens, the storehouse of his bounty, to send rain on your land in season and to bless all the work of your hands" (Deut. 28:12).

Notice that the "storehouse" of God's "bounty" or blessing is "rain . . . in season"—not sunshine. (Perhaps it is easier to understand if you remember that sunny weather was the rule to which rain was a blessed exception rather than rainy weather being the rule with sunshine being the happy deviation. Palestine was and is a land of sunshine to which rain is added as a perk, not vice versa. So with rain being the anomaly, so to speak, it came to have singular importance.)

But if God's people neglected Him and did evil, Moses went on, then "the Lord will turn the rain of your country into dust and powder" (verse 24). In other words, the sun would shine relentlessly, searing and parching everything. As a result, there would be only one season (not two) in Palestine—the dry season.

Let me reemphasize the connection made here in Deuteronomy between climate and behavior. According to this model, God would bestow the rain upon His *obedient* people—the good—but He would bestow blistering sunshine upon His *disobedient* people—the bad.

It becomes easy to see, then, why abundance of rain stood for God's favor and abundance of sun connoted His disfavor. "Sin and drought were a continuum, the former begetting the latter and the latter certifying the former. . . . Control over rain . . . was equally control over sin and evil" *(ibid.,* p. 141).

We find the pattern running throughout Scripture. This Deuteronomistic theology "took"—it became a widespread motif in the Bible. So for the moment, let's concentrate solely on the alternation of rain (blessing) and no rain (cursing) in God's Word.

Still within the Pentateuch, we read: *"If you follow my decrees* and are careful to obey my commands, *I will send you rain* in its season, and the ground will yield its crops and the trees of the field their fruit" (Lev. 26:3, 4).

Much later, upon the deaths of King Saul and his son Jonathan, David's bosom buddy, David lamented: "O mountains of Gilboa, may you have neither dew nor rain, nor fields that yield offerings of grain. For there the shield of the mighty was defiled" (2 Sam. 1:21).

David's son Solomon offered a special prayer at the dedication of the magnificent Temple that he erected. Among other things, Solomon was concerned about possible rebellion and its results, and potential repentance and its consequences. So he prayed: "When the heavens are shut up and *there is no rain because your people have sinned* against you, and when they pray toward this place and confess your name and turn from their sin because you have afflicted them, *then hear* from heaven *and forgive* the sin of your servants, your people Israel. Teach them the right way to live, *and send rain* on the land you gave your people for an inheritance" (1 Kings 8:35, 36; see also 2 Chron. 6:26, 27).

After Solomon went to bed that night, God appeared to him and reassured him with these words: "When I shut up the heavens so that there is no rain . . . if my people, who are called by my name, will humble themselves and pray and seek my face and turn from their wicked ways, then will I hear from heaven and will forgive their sin and will heal their land" (2 Chron. 7:13, 14).

More years went by and King Ahab became notorious for his apostasy, which his wife Jezebel aided and abetted. So "Elijah the Tishbite . . . said to Ahab, 'As the Lord, the God of Israel, lives, whom I serve, there will be *neither dew nor rain* in the next few years except at my word'" (1 Kings 17:1).

The psalmist had earlier reiterated the idea that rain equaled blessing. "You gave abundant showers, O God; you refreshed your weary inheritance" (Ps. 68:9).

And the prophets agreed.

As far as biblical scholars can determine, Amos was the first prophet to write down his messages (the others had been preserved by memory for many years before being committed to writing). When Amos confronted the wickedness of the Israelites, he resorted to name calling. "Hear this word, you cows of Bashan on Mount Samaria, you women who oppress the poor and crush the needy. . . . The Sovereign Lord has sworn by his holiness: 'The time will surely come when you will be taken away with hooks, the last of you with fishhooks. . . . You will be cast out. . . . I gave you empty stomachs in every city and lack of bread in every town, yet you have not returned to me,' declares the Lord. *I also withheld rain* from you when the harvest was still three months away. I sent rain on one town, but withheld it from another. One field had rain; another had none and dried up'" (Amos 4:1-7).

After Amos the prophet, Hosea gave his messages to the nation of Israel. He also spoke of metaphorical rain. "Let us acknowledge the Lord. . . . As surely as the sun rises, he will appear; *he will come to us like the winter rains, like the spring rains* that water the earth" (Hosea 6:3). Spiritual preparation for God's blessings he likened to agricultural preparation: "Sow for yourselves righteousness, reap the fruit of unfailing love, and break up your unplowed ground; for it is time to seek the Lord, until he comes and *showers righteousness on you*" (Hosea 10:12).

Isaiah portrayed to his idolatrous compatriots what would happen when they turned from worshiping their false gods and once again began worshiping YHWH, the God of heaven. "Then you will defile your idols . . . and your images . . . ; you will throw them away like a menstrual cloth and say to them, 'Away with you!' *He will also send you rain* for the seed you sow in the ground, and the food that comes from the land will be rich and plentiful" (Isa. 30:22, 23; see also Isa. 5:6; 24:4; 44:3; 45:8; 55:10).

The prophet Joel addressed the nation of Judah, pointing

out God's abundant blessing of good (rainy) weather. "Be glad, O people of Zion, rejoice in the Lord your God, for *he has given you the autumn rains* in righteousness. He sends you *abundant showers*, both autumn and spring rains. . . . The threshing floors will be filled with grain; the vats will overflow with new wine and oil" (Joel 2:23, 24).

Jeremiah pointed out why God's people were suffering from a severe drought. "The *showers have been withheld*, and *no spring rains* have fallen. Yet you have the brazen look of a prostitute; you refuse to blush with shame," the prophet scolded (Jer. 3:3).

But Jeremiah was not content merely to define the problem to his friends. He turned to God and pleaded with Him, because the situation had become desperate. "The ground is cracked because *there is no rain* in the land; the farmers are dismayed and cover their heads. . . . Although *our sins testify against us,* O Lord, do something for the sake of your name. For our backsliding is great; we have sinned against you" (Jer. 14:4-7; see also Jer. 5:24).

Zechariah projected the Deuteronomistic theology onto other nations. He anticipated a worldwide revival in which the Gentiles would turn to the God of Israel. "If any of the peoples of the earth *do not go up to Jerusalem* to worship the King, the Lord Almighty, they will have *no rain*" (Zech. 14:17). Apparently the prophet did not worry about how this would take place in moderate climates outside subtropical Palestine!

Perhaps in church you have sung the gospel song "Showers of Blessing." Author Daniel W. Whittle got that expression from the prophet Ezekiel, who quoted God as saying: "I will bless them and the places surrounding my hill. I will send down showers in season; there will be showers of blessing" (Eze. 34:26).

Even the New Testament echoes this understanding. In the very last book of the Bible, John the revelator describes a period of apostasy when God's "two witnesses" would be harassed. "These men have power to shut up the sky so that *it will not rain* during the time they are prophesying" (Rev. 11:6).*

In addition to this pattern of rain being a blessing and no rain being a curse, notice the flip side of this coin—scorching sun indicates God's curse upon the disobedient and the absence of a parching sun is a blessing.

The psalmist, in speaking of God's protection upon His good people, sang: "The sun will not harm you" (Ps. 121:6).

Similarly, the prophet Isaiah predicted that God would protect His good people from too much sunshine: "They will neither hunger nor thirst, nor will the desert heat or the sun beat upon them. He who has compassion on them will guide them and lead them beside springs of water" (Isa. 49:10).

Jesus told a story about a garden destroyed by sunshine. "But when the sun came up, the plants were scorched, and they withered because they had no root" (Mark 4:6).

And James wrote about the sunny dry season. "For the sun rises with scorching heat and withers the plant; its blossom falls and its beauty is destroyed. In the same way, the rich man will fade away even while he goes about his business" (James 1:11).

Compare also the following observations from the last book of the Bible.

At the end of time, just prior to Jesus' second coming, one of the seven last plagues will affect the sun so that the bad people will suffer. "The fourth angel poured out his bowl on the sun, and the sun was given power to scorch people with fire" (Rev. 16:8).

However, God's good people—the redeemed—will no longer suffer under the annual drought that parched the Holy Land. "Never again will they hunger; never again will they thirst. The sun will not beat upon them, nor any scorching heat" (Rev. 7:16).

The pattern is clear. According to Deuteronomistic theology, (1) abundant rain blesses the obedient but (2) abundant sun shrivels the disobedient.

---

*We find four exceptions to this general rule that abundant rain means divine blessing on obedience.

First, there is the Noachian flood, in which God destroyed the world with a deluge of rain.

Second, Samuel predicted a destructive rain. But notice that in this instance the (latter) rain fell during the time of harvest, which thus substantiates the overall picture of the climate and the critical aspect of timing. "'Is it not wheat harvest now? I will call upon the Lord to send thunder and rain. And you will realize what an evil thing you did in the eyes of the Lord when you asked for a king.' Then Samuel called upon the Lord, and that same day the Lord sent thunder and rain. So all the people stood in awe of the Lord and of Samuel" (1 Sam. 12:17, 18).

Ezekiel described two destructive storms. The first storm is our third example. "The Sovereign Lord says: In my wrath I will unleash a violent wind, and in my anger . . . torrents of rain will fall with destructive fury" (Eze. 13:13).

And in the fourth example, Ezekiel speaks of a deluge that thwarts the hostile intent of Gog and Magog. "I will execute judgment upon him with plague and bloodshed; I will pour down torrents of rain, hailstones and burning sulfur on him and on his troops and on the many nations with him" (Eze. 38:22).

These four exceptions really tend to "prove the rule" that we've illustrated: rainy weather is good weather except for these four rare instances.

## WHEN GOD'S HEART BREAKS:

*"'For your Maker is your husband—the Lord Almighty*
*is his name. . . . With everlasting kindness I will have*
*compassion on you,' says the Lord*
*your Redeemer" (Isa. 54:5-8).*

# CHAPTER NINE

## The Other Shoe Drops

Eighth grade. 1955. Several remarkable events occurred in my life.

First, during the school Christmas program I sang "O Holy Night." The song had always been one of my favorites, and I looked forward to presenting it. However, during practice my voice kept cracking because my adolescent voice transformation was at its peak. I explained to my teacher, whom I loved and respected deeply, that I couldn't do the song. He pleaded, and I caved in. That night I was mortified as I yodeled through "O Holy Night."

As a result I vowed that I'd never sing a solo in public again. Some 40 years later my vow remains intact!

Second, prior to graduation I had my first shave. I couldn't find a whole lot, of course, to take off, but my face had sprouted sufficient fuzz that I used a borrowed electric razor for this significant milestone.

Third, charcoal-gray suits, pink shirts, and pink-and-gray bow ties were the rage. Mother thought I'd look stunning in such getup at my graduation. I loudly protested that pink was something girls and sissies wore. But because I didn't control the finances, I ended up looking like a sissy at my elementary school graduation. Mother proclaimed that I looked chic. My feelings were that you could add the letter k to that word in order to describe what I looked like. Yes, a chick! I felt disgraced.

Fourth, I learned a new word that school year—*synecdoche*.

Mr. Gray, who was clearly the finest elementary school teacher I'd had, had been an English major and took pains to ingrain in his pupils the fine points of grammar, syntax, and vocabulary. The word "synecdoche," he explained, was a literary term that described a figure of speech in which a part of the whole substituted for the entirety. Consider, for example, the following sentence: "Eighteen-year-old George was thrilled with his first set of wheels." The expression "set of wheels" is a synecdoche for automobile. A car consists of far more than wheels, but the part here (set of wheels) stands for the whole (car).

The expression "sunshine and rain" in the previous chapter—and in Scripture—is likewise a synecdoche. It made up merely a portion of either the blessings or terrible things that would happen to ancient Israel, depending on its corporate faithfulness to the covenant. Yes, rain versus sunshine was simply a part representing a much greater whole. According to Deuteronomistic theology, God would pour out *additional blessings* upon His good people and *other curses* would devastate His bad people.

Moses highlighted a long list of blessings that would be showered (significant term, don't you think?) upon God's good people. "If you fully obey the Lord your God and carefully follow all his commands I give you today, the Lord your God will set you high above all the nations on earth. All these blessings will come upon you and accompany you if you obey the Lord your God" (Deut. 28:1, 2).

The list of benefits included:

1. Blessed in the city (verse 3).
2. Blessed in the country (verse 3).
3. Offspring blessed (verse 4).
4. Crops blessed (verse 4).
5. Offspring of animals blessed (verse 4).
6. Basket and kneading trough blessed (verse 5).
7. Blessed coming and going (verse 6).
8. Enemies routed and defeated (verse 7).
9. Barns blessed (verse 8).
10. Everything you do blessed (verse 8).

11. All nations fear God's people (verse 10).
12. Abundant prosperity (verse 11).
13. Rain in its season (verse 12).
14. Always lending and never borrowing (verse 12).
15. Always head, not tail (verse 13).
16. Always at top, never at bottom (verse 13).

Moses didn't stop there with positive reinforcements for good behavior. God had negative reinforcements that He could use should His people lapse into bad behavior. "However, if you do not obey the Lord your God and do not carefully follow all his commands and decrees I am giving you today, all these curses will come upon you and overtake you" (Deut. 28:15).

The baneful list that followed was pretty much a mirror image of the blessings, but longer. It included:

1. Cursed in the city (verse 16).
2. Cursed in the country (verse 16).
3. Basket and kneading trough cursed (verse 17).
4. Offspring cursed (verse 18).
5. Crops cursed (verse 18).
6. Offspring of animals cursed (verse 18).
7. Cursed coming and going (verse 19).
8. Everything you do cursed (verse 20).
9. Destroyed with sudden ruin (verse 20).
10. Cursed with diseases (verses 21, 22).
    a. consumption
    b. fever
    c. inflammation
11. Cursed with heat and drought (verse 22).
12. Cursed with blight and mildew (verse 22).
13. Cursed with no rain (verse 24).
14. Defeated by enemies (verse 25).
15. Carcasses food for scavengers (verse 26).
16. Cursed with illnesses (verses 27, 28).
    a. boils
    b. tumors
    c. sores
    d. itch

    e. madness

    f. blindness

17. Cursed with failure (verse 29).
18. Be oppressed and robbed (verse 29).
19. Suitors jilted by lovers (verse 30).
20. Build houses but not move in (verse 30).
21. Plant gardens but not eat from them (verse 30).
22. Food animals killed but not eat of them (verse 31).
23. Donkeys stolen (verse 31).
24. Sheep given to enemies (verse 31).
25. Children will be POWs (verses 32, 41).
26. Exile (verses 36, 37).
27. Cursed with locust plague (verses 38, 42).
28. Cursed with crop failures (verses 39, 40).
29. Foreigners rise; Israelites sink (verse 43).
30. Borrow but not lend (verse 44).
31. Foreigners will be the head; Israelites, the tail (verse 44).
32. Israelites will resort to cannibalism under siege (verses 53-57).

Moses continued: "If you do not carefully follow all the words of this law, which are written in this book, and do not revere this glorious and awesome name—the Lord your God—the Lord will send fearful plagues on you and your descendants, harsh and prolonged disasters, and severe and lingering illnesses. He will bring upon you all the diseases of Egypt that you dreaded, and they will cling to you. *The Lord will also bring on you every kind of sickness and disaster not recorded in this Book of the Law,* until you are destroyed" (verses 58-61).

"Just as it pleased the Lord to make you prosper and increase in number, so it will please him to ruin and destroy you" (verse 63). Yet the disobedient Israelites would not even succeed as POWs. They would be continually restless, wishing during the night that it was day, and longing during the day for it to be night (verse 67). The exodus would be reversed, and they would return in droves to Egypt, but even there they would be failures. "You will offer yourselves for sale to your enemies as male and female slaves, but no one will buy you" (verse 68).

Deuteronomistic theology is quite simple: Obey and be blessed; disobey and be cursed. It was also straightforward, containing no ameliorating clauses—no maybes or possibilities. Scripture presents it in stark black-and-white terms. The contingencies were all on Israel's part—the ifs: *If* they obeyed . . . , and *if* they disobeyed . . . On God's part the blessing or cursing inexorably followed.

When Joshua replaced Moses as Israel's prophetic leader, God instructed him: "Be careful to obey all the law my servant Moses gave you; do not turn from it to the right or to the left, that you may be successful wherever you go. Do not let this Book of the Law depart from your mouth; meditate on it day and night, so that you may be careful to do everything written in it. Then you will be prosperous and successful" (Joshua 1:7, 8).

Shortly before Joshua died he called the Israelites together and reiterated to them what God had told him at the outset of his leadership. "If you turn away and ally yourselves with the survivors of these nations that remain among you and if you intermarry with them and associate with them, then you may be sure that the Lord your God will no longer drive out these nations before you. Instead, they will become snares and traps for you, whips on your backs and thorns in your eyes, until you perish from this good land" (Joshua 23:12, 13).

Furthermore, "Not one of all the good promises the Lord your God gave you has failed. Every promise has been fulfilled. . . . But just as every good promise of the Lord your God has come true, so the Lord will bring on you all the evil he has threatened, until he has destroyed you from this good land he has given you. If you violate the covenant of the Lord your God, which he commanded you, . . . the Lord's anger will burn against you, and you will quickly perish from the good land he has given you" (verses 14-16).

The crowd of Israelites responded fervently, for they intended to obey God's every command, but Joshua warned them that their God was pretty fierce and that they were woefully weak. "You are not able to serve the Lord. He is a holy God; he is a jealous God. He will not forgive your rebellion and your sins. If you forsake the Lord and serve foreign gods, he will turn and bring disaster on you and make an end of you, after he has been good to you" (Joshua 24:19, 20).

The people responded as one: "We will serve the Lord our God and obey him" (verse 24). And the Israelites followed through on their good intentions. Not only did they serve YHWH during Joshua's life, but after his death they were obedient "throughout the lifetime . . . of the elders who outlived him and who had experienced everything the Lord had done for Israel" (verse 31).

But finally that older generation died out, and then came the time of the judges, "when everyone did as he saw fit" (Judges 21:25), a recurring theme in the book of Judges. Throughout the biblical book we find Israel backsliding and suffering oppression. "Then the Israelites did evil in the eyes of the Lord and served the Baals. They forsook the Lord, the God of their fathers, who had brought them out of Egypt. . . . They provoked the Lord to anger because they forsook him. . . . In his anger against Israel the Lord handed them over to raiders who plundered them. He sold them to their enemies all around, whom they were no longer able to resist. Whenever Israel went out to fight, the hand of the Lord was against them to defeat them, just as he had sworn to them. They were in great distress" (Judges 2:11-15).

Then the Lord would raise up "judges" who reformed His people, but their influence was merely transitory, and before long God's people were wallowing in evil again. "Whenever the Lord raised up a judge for them, he was with the judge and saved them out of the hands of their enemies as long as the judge lived; for the Lord had compassion on them as they groaned under those who oppressed and afflicted them. But when the judge died, the people returned to ways even more corrupt than those of their fathers. . . . They refused to give up their evil practices and stubborn ways. Therefore the Lord was very angry with Israel" (verses 18-20) because they had broken covenant with Him.

Chapter after chapter in Judges opens with the sad refrain:

"The people of Israel did what was evil in the sight of the Lord" (see 3:7, 12; 4:1; 6:1; 13:1). Those chapters that do not begin with such words relate a sordid tale of apostasy nonetheless. God's people would sin, be oppressed, cry to God, be delivered by a "judge," only to return to their evil ways upon the national deliverer's death.

The book of Ruth is not quite as explicit, but the story opens during the time of the judges. Elimelech and his wife, Naomi, and two boys had fled Israel because of a famine and had taken up residence in Moab. Elimelech and his two sons (now married) died in Moab, but widow Naomi "heard . . . that *the Lord had come to the aid* of his people by providing food for them," so she "and her daughters-in-law prepared to return home from there" (Ruth 1:6).

The prophet Samuel later stated: "Therefore the Lord, the God of Israel, declares: 'I promised that your [Eli's] house and your father's house would minister before me forever.' But now the Lord declares: 'Far be it from me! *Those who honor me I will honor, but those who despise me will be disdained*'" (1 Sam. 2:30).

In his farewell speech before anointing a king for God's people, Samuel reiterated the traditional Deuteronomistic theology.

First, he reminded the people of what had happened in the past. "But they forgot the Lord their God; so he sold them into the hand of Sisera, the commander of the army of Hazor, and into the hands of the Philistines and the king of Moab, who fought against them" (1 Sam. 12:9).

Second, the judge/prophet explained to the people what would befall them in the future. "If you fear the Lord and serve and obey him and do not rebel against his commands, and if both you and the king who reigns over you follow the Lord your God—good! But if you do not obey the Lord, and if you rebel against his commands, his hand will be against you, as it was against your fathers" (verses 14, 15).

And so Samuel concluded with an appeal: "But be sure to fear the Lord and serve him faithfully with all your heart; consider what great things he has done for you. Yet if you persist in doing evil, both you and your king will be swept away" (verses 24, 25).

Samuel proceeded to coronate King Saul, and the two of them—the old prophet and the young king—had a pretty stormy relationship. But finally "Saul died because he was unfaithful to the Lord; he did not keep the word of the Lord" (1 Chron. 10:13).

And so the books of Samuel, Kings, and Chronicles relate the same patterns. When Israel's and Judah's kings kept covenant with YHWH, they prospered, but when they turned to idolatry and immorality, the fortunes of the nation waned as enemies came in and oppressed God's people. If the nation repented, God responded to them, and prosperity once more returned.

David, Israel's second king, and the other psalmists knew the pattern well. The good person would be "blessed" and be "like a tree planted by streams of water, which yields its fruit in season and whose leaf does not wither. Whatever he does prospers" (Ps. 1:3). But not so with the wicked, who are like wind-driven chaff—blown away (verse 4). "For the Lord watches over the way of the righteous, but the way of the wicked will perish" (verse 6).[1]

And here is that verse that Ed mentioned during my seminar on suffering. "I have never seen the righteous forsaken or their children begging bread. They are always generous and lend freely; their children will be blessed" (Ps. 37:25, 26).

The message comes through loud and clear in the psalms. Those who do good will have good things done to them, but those who do bad will experience bad things. It was the way that God reinforced His covenant with His people and was seen as a kind of spiritual discipline.

In the collection of Hebrew proverbs (many attributed to Solomon, David's son), we find a similar assumption.

"[The wicked] lie in wait for their own blood; they waylay only themselves! Such is the end of all who go after ill-gotten gain; it takes away the lives of those who get it" (Prov. 1:18, 19).

By way of contrast, God "is a shield to those whose walk is blameless, for he guards the course of the just and protects the way of his faithful ones" (Prov. 2:7, 8). They alone will inherit the land (verse 21).

Those who heed the instruction encapsulated in the Hebrew

proverbs will be blessed with a "life [of] many years" and "prosperity" (Prov. 3:2).[2]

And what about the kings that followed Saul and David? The same pattern holds.

"When the time drew near for David to die, he gave a charge to Solomon his son. 'I am about to go the way of all the earth,' he said. 'So be strong, show yourself a man, and observe what the Lord your God requires: Walk in his ways, and keep his decrees and commands, his laws and requirements, as written in the Law of Moses, so that you may prosper in all you do and wherever you go'" (1 Kings 2:1-3).

God, in talking to Solomon, reinforced what David had counseled. "And if you walk in my ways and obey my statutes and commands as David your father did, I will give you a long life" (1 Kings 3:14).

Solomon went on to construct a temple to YHWH, and as we saw earlier in this chapter, during his dedicatory prayer his words show that he was thoroughly indoctrinated in Deuteronomistic theology. (Since we cited parts of the prayer in our discussion about the rain, we will not repeat the passage here.)

And that evening God reminded King Solomon of the binding nature of Deuteronomistic theology. "As for you, if you walk before me in integrity of heart and uprightness, as David your father did, and do all I command and observe my decrees and laws, I will establish your royal throne over Israel forever. . . . But if you or your sons turn away from me and do not observe the commands and decrees I have given you and go off to serve other gods and worship them, then I will cut off Israel from the land I have given them and will reject this temple I have consecrated for my Name. Israel will then become a byword and an object of ridicule among all peoples. And though this temple is now imposing, all who pass by will be appalled and will scoff and say, 'Why has the Lord done such a thing to this land and to this temple?' People will answer, 'Because they have forsaken the Lord their God, who brought their fathers out of Egypt, and have embraced other gods, worshiping and serving them—that is why the Lord brought all this disaster on them'" (1 Kings 9:4-9).

And sure enough, that is precisely what happened during the reigns of Solomon's successors.

God told the prophet Ahijah: "Go, tell Jeroboam that this is what the Lord, the God of Israel, says: 'I raised you up from among the people and made you a leader over my people Israel. . . . But you have not been like my servant David, who kept my commands and followed me with all his heart, doing only what was right in my eyes. You have done more evil than all who lived before you. You have made for yourself other gods. . . . Because of this, I am going to bring disaster on the house of Jeroboam. I will cut off from Jeroboam every last male in Israel—slave or free. I will burn up the house of Jeroboam as one burns dung, until it is all gone'" (1 Kings 14:7-10).[3]

During Jeroboam's reign, God fought against King Abijah. "The men of Israel were subdued on that occasion, and the men of Judah were victorious because they relied on the Lord, the God of their fathers" (2 Chron. 13:18).

Under King Rehoboam the same pattern held. So it didn't matter whether one was in Israel or Judah. Deuteronomistic theology continued to be the conventional wisdom. "Judah did evil in the eyes of the Lord. By the sins they committed they stirred up his jealous anger more than their fathers had done." So "in the fifth year of King Rehoboam, Shishak king of Egypt attacked Jerusalem. He carried off the treasures of the temple of the Lord and the treasures of the royal palace. He took everything, including all the gold shields Solomon had made. . . . There was continual warfare between Rehoboam and Jeroboam" (1 Kings 14:22-30).

God spoke through Jehu to King Baasha, and the message was the same. "I lifted you up from the dust and made you leader of my people Israel, but you walked in the ways of Jeroboam and caused my people Israel to sin and to provoke me to anger by their sins. So I am about to consume Baasha and his house, and I will make your house like that of Jeroboam son of Nebat" (1 Kings 16:2, 3).[4]

Later on King Ahab reveled in apostasy. "Now Elijah the Tishbite . . . said to Ahab, 'As the Lord, the God of Israel, lives, whom I serve, there will be neither dew nor rain in the next few years except at my word'" (1 Kings 17:1).

After the long drought, Elijah confronted Ahab again. But "Ahab said to Elijah, 'So you have found me, my enemy!' 'I have found you,' he answered, 'because you have sold yourself to do evil in the eyes of the Lord. "I am going to bring disaster on you. I will consume your descendants and cut off from Ahab every last male in Israel—slave or free"'" (1 Kings 21:20, 21).[5]

Fortunately, Hezekiah was a good king. "Hezekiah trusted in the Lord, the God of Israel. There was no one like him among all the kings of Judah, either before him or after him. He held fast to the Lord and did not cease to follow him; *he kept the commands* the Lord had given Moses. And *the Lord was with him;* he was successful in whatever he undertook" (2 Kings 18:5-7).[6]

But King Manasseh reverted to the tradition of being a bad king. "Manasseh king of Judah has committed these detestable sins. He has done more evil than the Amorites who preceded him and has led Judah into sin with his idols. Therefore this is what the Lord, the God of Israel, says: I am going to bring such disaster on Jerusalem and Judah that the ears of everyone who hears of it will tingle. I will stretch out over Jerusalem the measuring line used against Samaria and the plumb line used against the house of Ahab. I will wipe out Jerusalem as one wipes a dish, wiping it and turning it upside down. I will forsake the remnant of my inheritance and hand them over to their enemies. They will be looted and plundered by all their foes, because they have done evil in my eyes and have provoked me to anger from the day their forefathers came out of Egypt until this day" (2 Kings 21:11-15).[7]

King Zedekiah was not much of an improvement. "He did evil in the eyes of the Lord, just as Jehoiakim had done. It was because of the Lord's anger that all this happened to Jerusalem and Judah, and in the end he thrust them from his presence" (2 Kings 24:19, 20).[8]

During the monarchies, the prophets in their messages upheld Deuteronomistic theology.

Isaiah quoted God as saying: "The earth is defiled by its people; they have disobeyed the laws, violated the statutes and broken the everlasting covenant. Therefore a curse consumes the earth; its people must bear their guilt. Therefore earth's inhabitants are burned up, and very few are left. The new wine dries up and the vine withers; all the merrymakers groan" (Isa. 24:5-7).

"If only you had paid attention to my commands, your peace would have been like a river, your righteousness like the waves of the sea. Your descendants would have been like the sand, your children like its numberless grains; their name would never be cut off nor destroyed from before me" (Isa. 48:18, 19).[9]

Jeremiah took up the same refrain. "Look up to the barren heights and see. Is there any place where you have not been ravished? . . . You have defiled the land with your prostitution and wickedness. Therefore the showers have been withheld, and no spring rains have fallen" (Jer. 3:2, 3).

"Walk in all the ways I command you, that it may go well with you" (Jer. 7:23).[10]

When God's people entered Babylonian exile after God's "servant" Nebuchadnezzar conquered them, Ezekiel reiterated the message. "Therefore this is what the Sovereign Lord says: You have been more unruly than the nations around you and have not followed my decrees or kept my laws. You have not even conformed to the standards of the nations around you. Therefore this is what the Sovereign Lord says: I myself am against you, Jerusalem, and I will inflict punishment on you in the sight of the nations" (Eze. 5:7, 8).[11]

And Daniel, Ezekiel's contemporary and one of the first prisoners of war Nebuchadnezzar took to Babylon, agreed with this Deuteronomistic perspective. "We have not obeyed the Lord our God or kept the laws he gave us through his servants the prophets. All Israel has transgressed your law and turned away, refusing to obey you. Therefore the curses and sworn judgments written in the Law of Moses, the servant of God, have been poured out on us, because we have sinned against you" (Dan. 9:10, 11).

Hosea, the first of the so-called minor prophets, sang the same refrain. " 'Ephraim is blighted, their root is withered, they yield no fruit. Even if they bear children, I will slay their cherished offspring. My *God will reject them because they have not obeyed* him; they will be wanderers among the nations" (Hosea 9:16, 17).[12]

Deuteronomistic theology became all-pervasive in ancient Israel—probably because it made so much common sense. God sets out rules for His people, takes them seriously, and wants His people to do the same. To reinforce the importance of His laws, He will bless those who adhere to them and curse those who reject them. Thus despite its protological thinking, ancient Israel saw a cause-and-effect relationship between obedience and benefit, disobedience and affliction.

Additionally, such a philosophy corresponded well with other areas of life. Pretty much everything that made life pleasant—or at least tolerable—had to be "earned." The people won barley and wheat and olives and grapes from the earth by horticultural techniques. Bread was kneaded from flour that was ground from the grain that had been threshed from the harvested stalks.

Sheep and goats and cows and donkeys were produced by the techniques of husbandry. Clothing and shelter came the hard way—by cutting it off the sheep and goats and carding and spinning and weaving it—or by scraping animal hides and tanning them. Or by chiseling stone from quarries and lugging it to building sites.

And life is pretty much the same today. We merit our job titles and positions and earn our paychecks. In school we study hard to earn good grades. All in all, we get what we deserve. As Max Lucado has pointed out: "You work hard, you pay your dues, and 'zap'—your account is credited as paid in full" *(The Applause of Heaven,* p. 31). So we get merit raises . . . and deserve a break today!

Why shouldn't religion be the same way, especially when God so closely tied it to material "blessings" (go back to the list of blessings above—how many of them are material and how many spiritual?)? According to Deuteronomy, God's people would get what they earned. If they obeyed Him, they would merit blessing. But if they disobeyed Him, they would deserve the curses coming their way.

Probably another reason that this theology caught on among

God's ancient people was because it more or less followed the pattern employed in ancient suzerainty treaties, as many scholars have pointed out. Legislative codes with sanctions such as blessings and cursings formed part of the pattern used in covenant treaties that aligned one group of people with a particular monarch.

Because God's code with ancient Israel tracked this common practice, it would have struck a responding chord with Israel. Such an approach was, to use a contemporary term, politically correct!

Finally, Deuteronomistic theology likely "took" because the concept of a god reenforcing human behavior with a carrot or a stick was commonplace—an early form of behaviorism, perhaps. This philosophy permeated the ancient Near East, as is well attested in documents uncovered by archaeologists and deciphered by linguists.

In **Egypt** Wen-Amon, a high-ranking official of the Temple of Amon at Karnak, wrote in the eleventh century B.C. about a trip he made to Byblos. Among his observations was the following: "Now as for Amon-Re, King of the Gods—he is the lord of this life and health. . . . *If you say* to Amon: 'Yes, *I will do (it)!*' and you carry out his commission, *you will live, you will be prosperous, you will be healthy" (The Ancient Near East,* vol. 1, p. 21; italics supplied).[13]

**Mesopotamia** had an old proverb: "Do [no] evil, then you will [not] clutch a lasting [sorr]ow" *(ibid.,* p. 244).

**Akkadian** King Ashurnirari V of Assyria cut a covenant with King Mati'ilu of Arpad. The sacrificial lamb slain to ratify the covenant was said to represent King Mati'ilu, and what happened to the lamb would surely occur to the vassal king if he did not obey the provisions of the treaty.

And if Mati'ilu did not remain loyal to King Ashurnirari V (in other words, obey him), dire consequences would descend upon the disobedient vassal. The gods would impose sanctions. "May the great lord Sin . . . clothe Mati'ilu, his sons, his officials, and the people of his land in leprosy as in a cloak. . . . Let there be no milk. . . . May Adad . . . put an end to Mati'ilu, his land and the people of his land through hunger, want, and famine, so that they eat the flesh of their sons and daughters and it taste as good to them as the flesh of spring lambs. May they be deprived of Adad's thunder so that rain be denied them. . . . Let the farmers of his land not sing the harvest song in the fields, no vegetation should spring forth . . . and see the sunlight, [the . . .] not draw water from the springs. . . . Then may Ashur . . . turn your land into wasteland . . . , your cities into ruin mounds. . . . May Mati'ilu's [seed] be that of a mule, his wives barren. . . . May [locusts] appear and devour his land, may [. . .] blind their eyes" *(ibid.,* vol. 2, pp. 50, 51).[14]

**Assyrian** Yahdun-Lim dedicated a temple to Shamash at Mari by writing on nine bricks. Good people would not, of course, desecrate the temple, but bad people might. "Whoever desecrates this temple . . . or prompts someone else to . . . , be this man a king, or a general, or a mayor, or whoever else . . . Enlil . . . should make the kingdom of this man smaller than that of all the other kings; Sin [the moon god] . . . should curse him with the 'Great Curse'; Nergal . . . should break his weapon. . . . Ea . . . should make his fate a bad one; . . . Bunene . . . should end his life, eliminate every offspring of his" *(ibid.,* p. 96).

At Atchana in **Syria** a statue of King Idrimi of Alalakh seated on his throne bore an inscription engraved by Sharruwa. "May the god of heaven extirpate every offspring of whosoever steals this statue of mine, and curse him, extirpate his sons and offspring also of his . . . servants. . . . May the gods of heaven . . . keep the scribe Sharruwa who has written [the text of] this statue in good health and protect him" *(ibid.,* p. 99).

**Babylonian** Adad-guppi, the mother of King Nabonidus, who was the father of the biblical Belshazzar, had a lengthy inscription placed on her tomb. Worshiping the moon god Sin all her life (having taken refuge in him from childhood), she described herself as having "been piously devoted all my lifetime to Sin." And she lived to be 95 years old—an extraordinarily old age when most women died young, usually in childbirth.

As a result she believed that Sin had blessed her because of her devotion to him. "He looked with favor upon my pious good works and listened to my prayers, accepted my vows." The god Sin elevated her son Nabonidus to kingship. Additionally,

"Sin . . . did what he had not done before, had not granted to anybody else, he gave me (a woman) an exalted position and a famous name. . . . He added (to my life) many days (and) years of happiness. . . . My eyesight was good (to the end of my life), my hearing was excellent, my hands and feet were sound, my words well chosen, food and drink agreed with me, my health was fine and my mind happy. I saw my great-great-grandchildren, up to the fourth generation, in good health and (thus) had my fill of old age" *(ibid.,* pp. 106, 107).

**Aramaic** Ahiqar, who lived in the fifth century B.C., wrote the story of his life, along with some wisdom that he had gained. Among other things, he observed: "He with whom God is, who ca[n cas]t him down?" *(ibid.,* vol. 1, p. 249).

You get the point. The other nations had a theology quite reminiscent of the Deuteronomistic theology that Moses propounded.

James M. Scott discusses this Deuteronomistic theological perspective in the *Journal of Biblical Literature.* He points out that this concept "permeated virtually all extant literature and covered the whole history of Israel from initial election to ultimate salvation" ("Paul's Use of Deuteronomic Tradition," *JBL* 112, No. 4 [Winter 1993]: 647).

Scott refers to the formula **S E R**—sin, exile, restoration. Joseph Klausner, he points out, uses the formula **S P R R**—sin, punishment, repentance, redemption *(ibid.,* p. 650, note 21).

Although Scott sees this "Deuteronomic View of Israel's History" as relatively late, covering a period of three centuries from 200 B.C. to A.D. 100, those of us with a more conservative bent would suggest that the theology goes back much, much further, pervading the entire Old Testament corpus.

Clearly this theology, rooted in the book of Deuteronomy, thoroughly permeated Old Testament Judaism. It pervaded the Torah, saturated the historic books, and suffused throughout the psalms and proverbs. Even the prophetic voices were redolent with it.

---

[1] Here are more examples from Psalms: Ps. 5:4, 11, 12; 11:7; 16:3, 4;

24:5; 31:19; 32:10; 34:9, 10; 37:37, 38; 52:3-6; 67:6; 75:10; 91; 92:12-14; 112:1-3; 125:4, 5; and 145:20.

¹²Here are more examples from Proverbs: Prov. 3:33; 8:18, 20, 21; 10:2, 3, 27, 30; 13:25; 15:3; 16:20; 17:13, 20; 21:21; 22:4, 8; 24:20; 28:20; and 29:14.

³Ahijah had more to say; see 1 Kings 14:15.

⁴See also 1 Kings 16:12, 13, 18, 19.

⁵"All this took place because the Israelites had sinned against the Lord their God, who had brought them up out of Egypt from under the power of Pharaoh king of Egypt. They worshiped other gods" (2 Kings 17:7). See also verses 18, 19, 25.

⁶"This is what Hezekiah did throughout Judah, doing what was good and right and faithful before the Lord his God. In everything that he undertook in the service of God's temple and in obedience to the law and the commands, he sought his God and worked wholeheartedly. And so he prospered" (2 Chron. 31:20, 21).

⁷See also 2 Kings 22:16, 17; 24:3.

⁸The pattern continued. "Asa did what was good and right in the eyes of the Lord his God. . . . He built up the fortified cities of Judah, since the land was at peace. No one was at war with him during those years, for the Lord gave him rest" (2 Chron. 14:2-6).

"The Lord was with Jehoshaphat because in his early years he walked in the ways his father David had followed. He did not consult the Baals. . . . The Lord established the kingdom under his control; and all Judah brought gifts to Jehoshaphat, so that he had great wealth and honor" (2 Chron. 17:3-5).

"He sought God during the days of Zechariah, who instructed him in the fear of God. As long as he sought the Lord, God gave him success" (2 Chron. 26:5).

"Jotham grew powerful because he walked steadfastly before the Lord his God" (2 Chron. 27:6).

⁹See also Isa. 1:19, 20; 5:13; 9:19; 30:19-26.

¹⁰See also Jer. 5:24, 25; 9:12, 13; 11:7, 8; 16:4, 10-13; 17:4, 6-8, 27; 18:15-17; 19:3, 4, 8, 15; 21:5-7, 10; 22:4-9, 21; 23:14, 15; 24:9, 10; 25:5-11, 29; 29:17-19; 32:42; 34:17; and 35:17.

¹¹See also Eze. 5:12, 16, 17; 6:11; 9:9, 10; 14:13, 21; and 33:29.

¹²See also Hosea 2:3, 9; 4:6; and 9:15, 16.

¹³Ptah-hotep, the vizier of the Egyptian king Izezi of the Fifth Dynasty, around 2450 B.C. wrote down nuggets of wisdom for his own son. "There is punishment for him who passes over its laws. . . . Wrongdoing has never brought its undertaking into port. . . . Show regard for him in conformance with what has accrued to him—property does not come of itself. . . . It is god who makes (a man's) quality. . . . If a son accepts what his father says, no project of his miscarries. . . . (But) the induction of him who does not hearken miscarries" (*The Ancient Near East,* vol. 1, pp. 234-237).

"To put them in thy heart is worth while, (but) it is damaging to him who neglects them. . . . If thou spendest thy time while this is in thy heart, thou wilt find it a success; thou wilt find my words a treasury of life, and thy body will prosper upon earth. . . . He who does evil, the (very) river-bank abandons him, and his floodwaters carry him off. . . . As for the heated man of a temple, he is like a tree growing in the open. In the completion of a moment (comes) its loss of foliage, and its end is reached in the shipyards. . . . (But the truly silent man holds himself apart. He is like a tree growing in a garden. It flourishes and doubles its yield; . . . its fruit is sweet; its shade is pleasant; and its end is reached in the garden. . . . Do not cut off thy heart from thy tongue, that all thy affairs may be successful. . . . Make not for thyself weights which are deficient; they abound in grief through the will of god" *(ibid.,* pp. 237-241).

[14] Niqmepa, king of Alalakh and Mukishhe, imposed a treaty on King Ir-ⁿim of Tunip. The treaty has many provisions and ends by invoking the gods, who will enforce the treaty. "Whosoever transgresses these agreements, Adad, [. . .] and Shamash, the lord of judgment, Sin, and the great gods will make him perish" *(ibid.,* vol. 2, p. 48).

King Esarhaddon similarly established a covenant with King Baal of Tyre. Again the gods would enforce the sanctions. If Baal did not dutifully serve Esarhaddon, "may the Seven gods . . . cause your [downfall] with their [fierce] weapons. May Bethel and Anath-Bethel deliver you to a man-eating lion. . . . May the great gods . . . curse you with an indissoluble curse. . . . May Melqart and Eshmun deliver your land to destruction, your people to be deported. . . . May they make disappear food for your mouth, clothes for your body, oil for your ointment. . . . May a foreign enemy divide your belongings" *(ibid.,* p. 53).

The same Esarhaddon, "king of the world," set up vassal treaties with Ramataya, ruler of Urakazabanu. Once again the vassal must be obediently loyal, and once again the gods were called upon as punishers of disobedience. A list of sanctions followed. Here is just a sampling. "May Anu . . . rain upon all your houses disease, exhaustion, . . . sleeplessness, worries, ill health. . . . May Sin . . . clothe you in leprosy. . . . May Shamash . . . take away your eyesight. . . . May Ninurta . . . fill the plain with your corpses. . . . May Jupiter . . . put an end to your lives. . . . May Belet-ili . . . put an end to birth giving in your land. . . . May Adad . . . put an end [to vegetation] in your land . . . and hit your land with a severe destructive downpour, may locusts . . . [devour] your crops. . . . May the great gods of heaven and earth . . . look with disfavor upon you, curse you angrily with a baleful curse" *(ibid.,* pp. 62-64).

The Akkadian "Counsels of Wisdom" contain this insight: "Reverence begets favor, sacrifice improves life" *(ibid.,* p. 148).

# WHEN GOD'S HEART BREAKS:

*" 'Though the mountains be shaken and the hills be removed, yet my unfailing love for you will not be shaken . . . ,' says the Lord, who has compassion on you"* (Isa. 54:10).

# CHAPTER TEN

## The Rest of the Story

Have you ever listened to Paul Harvey on the radio? If so, you are acquainted with the feature he calls The Rest of the Story, during which he tells a story about a well-known person, but refers to the individual by a nickname so that it is not readily apparent whom he has in mind. After relating some intriguing tale about the individual, Paul Harvey then reveals the rest of the story—adding more familiar information and finally the full name. Aha! So that's whom he was referring to!

That's also what we sometimes find in the Bible. When Moses sent the 12 Israelite spies into the land of Canaan to reconnoiter the Promised Land, the majority report was not encouraging. Ten of the secret agents took a commonsense approach and advised not trying to conquer Canaan. The Israelites were outnumbered. Furthermore, giants dwelled in the land! When outnumbered by giants, it hardly seems prudent to pick a fight.

But then there's the rest of the story.

Two of the spies—Caleb and Joshua—encouraged the Israelites to move ahead with their plans. There was more to be said than simply what the 10 undercover agents reported. Israel *could* prevail—notwithstanding the size of the cities, the height and thickness of their city walls, or the build of the incredible hulks stomping around the countryside.

That's also sort of the way it is in Scripture when it comes to what we have been calling Deuteronomistic theology. Most of the Old Testament clearly indicates that goodness brings its own rewards and evilness reaps its own terrible harvest. But that is not all that the Scripture writers say about good and evil, crime and punishment, rain and sunshine, prosperity and adversity.

Once again there is the rest of the story. Occasionally—and apparently only occasionally—someone had more to say than had already (and traditionally) been presented.

The prophet Malachi quoted God and His people in conversation: "'You have said harsh things against me,' says the Lord. 'Yet you ask, "What have we said against you?" You have said, "It is futile to serve God. What did we gain by carrying out his requirements and going about like mourners before the Lord Almighty?"'" (Mal. 3:13, 14). Some felt that it was futile to serve God, because instead of being blessed they felt cursed.

Now according to the context, these were *rebellious* people complaining. What else should we expect from them? What about the rest of the story from those unflinchingly dedicated to YHWH?

Well, the author of Psalm 10 refused to let popular thought blind his eyes to the reality about him, and he said of the bad or wicked person: "His ways are always prosperous; he is haughty and your laws are far from him; he sneers at all his enemies" (verse 5). Here we find the rest of the story.

Clearly it did not take a genius to notice that bad people did *not* necessarily suffer. More had to be said than what one typically heard in the conventional wisdom.

However, the most gripping account of the rest of the story comes in the books of Job and Ecclesiastes.

Job, for instance, had a lot more to say about the human condition in the face of suffering than what his conservative friends propounded and what one can today read in those texts espousing Deuteronomistic theology.

The patriarch asserted his innocence again and again and bitterly complained that God had singled him out unfairly. "I despise my life; I would not live forever. Let me alone; my days have no meaning. What is man that you make so much of him, that you give him so much attention, that you examine him every morning and test him every moment? Will you never look away from me, or let me alone even for an instant? If I have sinned, what have I done to you, O watcher of men? Why have you made me your target? Have I become a burden to you? Why do you not pardon my offenses and forgive my sins? For I will soon lie down in the dust; you will search for me, but I will be no more" (Job 7:16-21).

Again: "Although I am blameless, I have no concern for myself; I despise my own life. It is all the same; that is why I say, *'He destroys both the blameless and the wicked.'* When a scourge brings sudden death, he mocks the despair of the innocent. When a land falls into the hands of the wicked, he blindfolds its judges. If it is not he, then who is it?" (Job 9:21-24).

Job insisted that God was unfair to him. "Know that God has wronged me and drawn his net around me. Though I cry, 'I've been wronged!' I get no response; though I call for help, there is no justice" (Job 19:6, 7).

"When I hoped for good, evil came; when I looked for light, then came darkness" (Job 30:26).[1]

And in the book of Ecclesiastes, which we conservative Christians consider to be just as inspired as the book of Deuteronomy, we find a less artful but nonetheless equally interesting account of the rest of the story. "Again I looked and saw all the oppression that was taking place under the sun: I saw the tears of the oppressed—and they have no comforter; power was on the side of their oppressors—and they have no comforter" (Eccl. 4:1).

According to the New International Version's rendition of the text, the author keeps referring to that which is "meaningless." The Hebrew word is not easily translated into sensible English. Its primary meaning is that of vapor. But talking about something being vaporous doesn't make much sense. The King James Version renders it "vanity." But that word has overtones of pride in contemporary English, and that's not what is signified here. The word might also be translated "absurd," which is getting pretty close to the intended meaning. "In this meaningless [absurd] life of mine I have seen both of these: a righteous man perishing in his righteousness, and a wicked man living long in his wickedness" (Eccl. 7:15).

"There is something else meaningless [absurd] that occurs on earth: righteous men who get what the wicked deserve, and wicked men who get what the righteous deserve. This too, I say, is meaningless" (Eccl. 8:14).

A little observation on the ancient author's part revealed that everyone—good and bad—had the same fate. So why bother? "So I reflected on all this and concluded that the righteous and the wise and what they do are in God's hands, but no man knows whether love or hate awaits him. All share a common destiny—the righteous and the wicked, the good and the bad, the clean and the unclean, those who offer sacrifices and those who do not. As it is with the good man, so with the sinner; as it is with those who take oaths, so with those who are afraid to take them. This is the evil in everything that happens under the sun: The same destiny overtakes all. The hearts of men, moreover, are full of evil and there is madness in their hearts while they live, and afterward they join the dead" (Eccl. 9:1-3).

Life was pretty macabre, and the author of Ecclesiastes, who Christians have traditionally felt was King Solomon, felt that it was an exercise in futility even to try to make sense of it all. "I have seen something else under the sun: The race is not to the swift or the battle to the strong, nor does food come to the wise or wealth to the brilliant or favor to the learned; but time and chance happen to them all" (verse 11).

"Sow your seed in the morning, and at evening let not your hands be idle, for you do not know which will succeed, whether this or that, or whether both will do equally well" (Eccl. 11:6).

The books of Job and Ecclesiastes were not alone in the ancient Near East in their renderings of the rest of the story. Although as pointed out earlier while the theological concept of "obey and be blessed; disobey and be cursed" was widespread, there were some ancient Paul Harveys outside Israel who also related the rest of the story.

A Babylonian parallel to the book of Job addressed the problem of suffering in an attempt to vindicate the gods. This

"Babylonian theodicy" is an acrostic poem of 27 stanzas, and each stanza consists of 11 lines. The acrostic itself reads: "I Saggil-kinam-ubbib, the exorcist, am an adorant of the god and the king."

In this treatise the sufferer complains, "Those who do not seek the god go the way of prosperity, while *those who pray* to the goddess *become destitute* and impoverished" (italics supplied)— an observation echoed in the biblical book of Ecclesiastes as well as in Job's speeches.

Furthermore, "the rich has only a carob to eat. The rich man is fallen"—something out of line with the traditional theological perspective. Moreover, "the god does not impede the way of even a demon. . . . *What has it profited me that I have bowed down to my god?*"

A friend of the ancient writer offers the insight that "you accuse the god wrongly. The mind of the god, like the center of the heavens, is remote; knowledge of it is very difficult; people cannot know it."

The text indicates that the complaints are not valid because what the young man grouses about are merely matters of appearance. And this appearance is not only superficial but quite transitory. "As for the rogue . . . his . . . soon vanishes. . . . Unless you seek the will of the god, what success can you have? He that bears his god's yoke never lacks food [remember Psalm 37:25?], even though it be sparse. . . . What you have lost in a year you will make up in a moment" if you "seek the favorable breath of the god" *(The Ancient Near East,* vol. 2, p. 165). Back to the conventional wisdom!

Also an unknown young man in ancient Sumeria wrote a treatise on suffering that likewise reminds one of the biblical book of Job. According to the theology presented in this ancient manuscript, suffering occurs because we all deserve it. Suffering is caused not by the gods *but by humans,* who thus get what they deserve.

But once sufferers discover their sins and repent of them, then their fortunes change. "My god, now that you have shown me my sins . . . I, the young man, would confess my sins before you. . . . The words which the young man prayerfully confessed, pleased the . . . flesh of his god, (and) his god withdrew his hand from the evil word, which oppresses the heart. . . . The encompassing sickness-demon, which had spread wide its wings, he swept away. . . . He turned the you[ng m]an's suffering into joy" (*ibid.,* pp. 140, 141).

Enough of opinion outside ancient Hebrew thought. What shall we say about this contrast between the "story" and the "rest of the story"—Deuteronomistic theology and the more that Scripture writers said? At this point, we need to remember the importance of focus.

First, we must keep in mind that theology *effects* religion. (Note the verb here. It is *effect,* which means to cause or produce.) A given theological emphasis brings about a specific religion. Calvinistic theology, with its focus on predestination, produced the Presbyterian religion, for instance. Luther's theology, with its emphasis on justification by grace alone, brought about the religion known as Lutheranism. Wesley's theology, with its stress on free will, spawned the religion of Methodism.

And so it was that the Deuteronomistic theology, with its focus on "obey and be blessed; disobey and be cursed," led to a religion that placed law central. In fact, the Hebrew term for law was Torah, and Torah became a shorthand word used to describe the entire corpus of the Hebrew sacred Scripture. We could fairly say that ancient Judaism was a juristic religion because of its focus on the law. Later this emphasis upon the Pentateuchal legislation became so important to some Jews that theologians have used the technical term "legalistic" (actually a synonym of juristic) to describe their religious expression.

Second, we can carry this a step further. Whereas theology *effects* religion, religion itself *affects* behavior. Note that the verb here is different. (It is *affect,* which means to influence.) In short, a religion motivates behavior and influences experience. In this instance, then, the Deuteronomistic theological focus of obey and live; disobey and die not only produced among some ancient

Jews a forensic religion, but it in turn had a tendency to modify behavior and experience in the direction of judgmentalism.

And why not? If one emphasizes that obedience brings blessing and disobedience leads to curses, then someone who is prospering (has plenty of money, good health, many offspring, etc.) is obviously good, because he or she is manifestly enjoying God's blessing. Similarly, someone who is not prospering (has poor health, poverty, and no children, etc.) is bad, because he or she is unquestionably suffering under God's displeasure.

So it was that Job's friends easily jumped to the conclusion that he was extraordinarily evil. After all, his children had all perished. His herds had all been destroyed. And he himself had come down with a loathsome disease. Nevertheless, Job had the audacity (in their opinion) to insist that he was good—not bad—and hence suffering unjustly. And so the bickering—rather, arguments—went back and forth. His friends got more strident, and he became more insistent in his protestations of innocence as the debate raged.

The same behavior (but its flip side) marked Jeremiah's compatriots, whom he criticized as being bad people in need of repentance. They countered that their behavior must not be all that bad, because they were doing quite well, thank you. On the other hand, when they had been scrupulously religious (read "obediently law-abiding"), things had gone poorly for them. Clearly, the kind of behavior Jeremiah urged brought God's displeasure, not His smile!

At issue was the idolatry of God's people. They, especially the women, had begun worshiping the queen of heaven—Ishtar (aka Ashtoreth). Jeremiah called for a halt of such idolatry. But . . .

"Then all the men who knew that their wives were burning incense to other gods . . . said 'We will not listen to the message you have spoken to us in the name of the Lord! . . . We will burn incense to the Queen of Heaven and will pour out drink offerings to her just as we and our fathers, our kings and our officials did in the towns of Judah and in the streets of Jerusalem. At that time we had plenty of food and were well off and suffered no harm. But ever since we stopped burning incense to the Queen of Heaven and pouring out drink offerings to her, we have had nothing and have been perishing by sword and famine" (Jer. 44:15-18).

Their behavior had indeed been affected by their religion, which had been effected by Deuteronomistic theology.

It is difficult not to become judgmental of others (as Job's friends were of him) or of oneself (as Jeremiah's compatriots were) when the espoused religion is juristic in focus and rooted in a theology of obey and God blesses; disobey and God curses.[2]

But that was then. What about now and our religion—Christianity?

Years ago I read somewhere that Christianity is the only world religion that has taken for its own Scripture the sacred writings of another religion. Yes, that is precisely what we've done. We've accepted the Old Testament (Judaism's Torah) and made it our own by adding to it what we call the New Testament.

It looks like a situation of "all this, *and* . . ." The "all this" is the Hebrew Scripture. The "and" in this instance, of course, is Jesus of Nazareth, whom we consider to be the Messiah (another Jewish concept), as well as the writings that He spawned—the New Testament's Gospels and Epistles and Apocalypse.

And there appears to be evidence to support this assumption of "all this, *and* . . ." Not only was Jesus a Jew, but many modern theologians are quite clear in their insistence that He was a *practicing* first-century Jew. Living in harmony with Jewish customs, He attended the synagogue on Sabbath and frequented the Temple when in Jerusalem.

His disciples were Jewish also, and after His ascension, those first Christians continued to go to the Temple, where they prayed as well as offered sacrifices. When traveling in the Diaspora, the early Christian missionaries not only attended the synagogues but also spoke in them. Other Jewish customs continued in the primitive Christian church—circumcision, tithing, clean/unclean distinctions in food, fast days, pledges.

So was Christianity little more than an extension of Judaism? A Judaism plus? A situation that exemplified "all this, *and* . . ."?

Not so fast. Other evidence clearly indicates that the situation was more likely that of "all this, *but . . .*" Once again, there is more to be said.

From the Gospel accounts of Jesus' life, we also gather that although Jesus may have been as practicing a Jew as the common people who "heard Him gladly," some of the scribes and Pharisees did not find Him an ideal follower of Judaism. He healed chronically ill people on the Sabbath. Jesus allowed His disciples to pick grain, thresh it in their hands, and eat it on the Sabbath. His disciples (and probably He Himself) did not wash their hands in the ceremonial ritual before dining. His daily associations with women, Samaritans, and publicans kept Him pretty much in a continual state of ritual impurity.

Paul even had more to say, carrying things even further. He downplayed kosher food (1 Cor. 8:1-13; 1 Tim. 4:3-5) despite the Jerusalem Council's minimal "Jewish" regulations that it felt all Christians needed to abide by. And he insisted that circumcision was no longer necessary. The apostle clearly indicated that when he was with Gentiles, he lived as they did as far as Jewish tradition was concerned (1 Cor. 9:21).

It ultimately became clear to both sides that Christianity was indeed a distinct religion. Probably this became obvious to Christians during the Bar Kosiba (Cochba) revolution (A.D. 132-135), when being labeled as Jewish by Rome was as popular as being labeled German during World War I. Some evidence suggests that around this time Christians began worshiping on Sunday. And the Jewish community may have also brought matters to a head when it inserted the *ha minim* (a curse on heretics and popularly perceived as referring to Christians) into the prayers repeated at the Sabbath synagogue service, thereby making it impossible for many Christians to participate. With these partings of the way, both communities of faith increasingly regarded each other as a separate and distinctive religion.

Well, this turned out to be a pretty long discussion. If you've stuck with me thus far, you may have forgotten the question that opened this whole discussion several chapters ago. Remember

Ed's question? He wanted to know what we should do about the psalmist's claim that he never saw the righteous begging for food and Malachi's argument that those who tithe faithfully will be extremely prosperous and have the "devourer" rebuked.

In the light of this discussion, I think we can raise a counterquestion: What did *Jesus* do with the two passages Ed cited? Since we are Christians—followers of Jesus Christ—His reaction should set a paradigm, or model, for us just as Moses' words established one for Israel.

The problem with our counterquestion is that we do not find a record in the four Gospels of Jesus citing either of those Old Testament verses that Ed mentioned. So is our counterquestion futile? Not at all—at least not if we rephrase our question. Let's ask it this way: How did Jesus relate to the Deuteronomistic theology that lay behind Psalm 37:25 and Malachi 3:10, 11?

That's a question we *can* answer. Jesus did have more to say (we are not necessarily talking word count here) than what one reads in passages such as Deuteronomy 28.

As we now take up the rest of the story as presented by Jesus, for the next few moments put yourself back in A.D. 27 or 28 or 29. You have grown up immersed in first-century Judaism. As a child you attended the synagogue schools, having sat at the feet of an eminent teacher of the Torah. In fact, much of your education required you to pretty much memorize the entire Mosaic law as well as scribal interpretations of it—*halakoth*.

Steeped in the history of the Israelites, you have read the psalms and proverbs and pondered the words of the *nebiim*—prophets. You have studied the vicissitudes of Israel's and Judah's fortunes: apostasy and disaster; reformation and prosperity. The last famous example of this—the Babylonian Exile—may have occurred hundreds of years earlier, but its lessons are fresh in your mind. "Never again," loyal first-century Jews insist. They will obey every jot and tittle of the law so that they will never again be deported to a distant and foreign land.

Thoroughly familiar with Deuteronomistic thought, you, along with most of your compatriots, believe "that sin is punished in this life. Every affliction [you regard] as the penalty of some wrongdoing, either of the sufferer himself or of his parents. . . . Hence one upon whom some great affliction or calamity had fallen had the additional burden of being regarded as a great sinner" (Ellen G. White, *The Desire of Ages,* p. 471).

In fact, because of this belief you could very well have posed the same question to Jesus that His disciples did when they encountered the man born blind: "Rabbi, who sinned, this man or his parents, that he was born blind?" (John 9:1).

Although you may not have intended to be harsh or judgmental, still your religious convictions would have pushed you to ask this question, which to you would have been completely logical and scriptural.

(Interestingly, this concept that sin receives its punishment in this life, that bad things happen to bad people, ended up hurting Jesus. "Thus the way was prepared for the Jews to reject Jesus. He who 'hath borne our griefs, and carried our sorrows' was looked upon by the Jews as 'stricken, smitten of God, and afflicted;' and they hid their faces from Him" *[ibid.]*).

But back to Jesus of Nazareth and His rest of the story. One sunny day you follow the crowds to a hillside where Jesus is addressing the people. You are enthralled with His words: "Blessed are the poor in spirit: for theirs is the kingdom of heaven. Blessed are they that mourn: for they shall be comforted. Blessed are the meek . . ." (Matt. 5:3-5, KJV).

You hang on every word. But then this same Jesus, who has been uttering such enrapturing thoughts, flings out a few zingers: "You may have heard that it was said . . . but I tell you . . ." (Matt. 5:21, 22, 27, 28, 31, 32, 33, 34, 38, 39, 43, 44). It appears to you that Jesus is taking potshots at Judaism's most treasured wisdom. Even more startling, He says: "He [Your Father in heaven] causes his sun to rise on the evil and the good, and sends rain on the righteous and the unrighteous" (verse 45). The blessing of rain on the evil, and the withholding of that blessing from the good? (Remember that while we think of getting rained on as bad, rain was considered a great good in Palestine.)

Stunned, your mind reels. Jesus' statement goes far beyond

the Deuteronomistic theology you learned in synagogue school. God sending the blessing of rain on the evil, and the curse of sun on the good? Not only that, but He sounds as though He perceives Himself to be another Moses. He has indicated that He had not come to destroy Torah but to fulfill it (verse 17), and at first you were able to give Him the benefit of the doubt, because when He had said "You've heard . . . but I say . . ." He was not so much doing away with Torah and halakah but spiritualizing them, applying them to the heart and mind rather than to mere overt actions.

But this new example seems to be different. You wrestle with His teaching. His focus seems to differ from that which you have learned. To you His teaching sounds like a kind of blasphemy. Who is this Jesus to apparently disagree with Moses—Moses, of all people?

But that is not all Jesus said about lifestyle and its reward here and now. There's even more—elsewhere. On another occasion here's what took place: "Now there were some present at that time who told Jesus about the Galileans whose blood Pilate had mixed with their sacrifices. Jesus answered, 'Do you think that these Galileans were worse sinners than all the other Galileans because they suffered this way? I tell you, no! But unless you repent, you too will all perish. Or those eighteen who died when the tower in Siloam fell on them—do you think they were more guilty than all the others living in Jerusalem? I tell you, no! But unless you repent, you too will all perish'" (Luke 13:1-5).

According to what you had always thought, the people who suffered such disasters must have been evil, because bad things happen to bad people and good things happen to good people. But Jesus insists that this is *not* the case. These victims were no more sinful than anyone else.

When you and other first-century Jews combine what He had to say here with His statements in Matthew, it becomes clear to you that Jesus' rest of the story is quite challenging and that He must be exceptionally brave. . . . Or unduly foolhardy.

You cannot help wondering. Just who is this young upstart,

anyway? Naive? Not really. Arrogant? Hardly. Deluded? No. God? Yes, Divinity incarnate, at least according to subsequent Christian thought. Later Christians came to believe that we get no more crystalline depiction of God than that provided by and in Jesus Christ Himself. But back to you, a first-century Jew. Jesus, whose words you've heard with your own ears, has ventured to say more about this terribly difficult topic than you had ever encountered before. And that disturbs you.

It surely must have been difficult for you and other first-century Jews to accept Jesus' theological emphasis. And today at the close of the twentieth century many of us still find it uncomfortable to accept this conclusion. We usually like to think that everything given by inspiration speaks with one voice and that uniformity of thought (and focus) marks all Scripture. But it does not appear that God whizzed all His spokespeople in some giant theological Osterizer.

Jesus appears to have concluded that much of what He and others had read in the Hebrew Scriptures was not all that should be said or needed to be said on the topic of obedience and prosperity versus disobedience and disaster.

First, Jesus *taught* what at least superficially the people of His time could have construed as a heterodox opinion. In addition to these forthright statements, which could hardly be more clear, He told stories that emphasized the same point of view. The most famous parable embracing Jesus' revolutionary concept was that of the prodigal son.

You recall the tale. The father capitulated to the son's selfish request and gave him his inheritance early. (In essence, the son was wishing his father had already died so that he could get his share of the estate. Estates were never divided up until the head of the household died.) The son then fled home, wasted his patrimony, and finally returned indigent and homeless.

When the father saw his errant son a long way off, he sprinted to greet him. (Ancient Near Easterners did not usually run because it revealed a lack of dignity.) Then the father threw a gala ball to celebrate his son's arrival.

The most shocking aspect of the story (as though what

we've reviewed already is not incredible enough) is that the father in the story epitomizes God! The prodigal son did not get what he deserved.

Second, Jesus also *lived* what He taught. Just as God sends rain and sunshine on both the good and the bad, so Jesus fellowshipped with the good and the bad—indiscriminately. Jesus did not discriminate when it came to taking meals. He dined with the Pharisees and ate with publicans. Jesus healed both an innocent 12-year-old girl and a man crippled from a life of dissipation. Furthermore, He jeopardized His community standing and honor by socializing with women—even women of ill repute.

Third, if you stop to think about it for a moment, what is one of the most common words used to describe Christian theological focus? Is it not the word "grace"? And grace means that sinners do not get what they deserve. Jesus incarnated grace.

The good news (that's what the word "gospel" literally means) is that God does not give us what we have coming. Instead, He treats us better than we merit. Indeed, He treats us as He treats Jesus Himself.

Jesus heralded a theology that emphasized grace, which later held Paul spellbound. The apostle's Epistles overflow with this "new" doctrine. (There are, of course, Old Testament roots to this emphasis also.) God's blessing of salvation comes not because we deserve it. We don't. All our adherence to legal niceties don't count one whit in God's sight, and Paul said that he regarded his former adherence to religious and legal fine points as "garbage" (Phil. 3:8, CEV).[3]

Let's return to a theme we noted earlier: theology *effects* or produces religion. And the religion that Jesus' theology of grace brought into existence is called Christianity. Relatively quickly it became obvious that what Jesus' theology led to was not another Jewish sectarian group but an altogether distinct religion—Christianity.

Thus despite the similarities between Judaism (rabbinic and modern) and Christianity, despite their common roots, and despite their respect for the same sacred canon (the Old Testament), there was still something rudimentarily different between them.

Again, as we noticed previously, religion *affects* or influences behavior. And the theology that Jesus put forward produces a religion that makes for nonlegalistic or nonjudgmental behavior (except when it is distorted by overly sensitive consciences). Christians, when they are true to the focus on grace that stands behind their religion (unfortunately, Christians do *not* always live in harmony with their theological ideals), are warmhearted individuals who are accepting (though not condoning) of all.

On the other hand, Deuteronomistic theology as too often understood was not conducive to producing great outreaches of altruism.[4] After all, when we regard disaster, disease, and death as either disciplinary or punitive measures from God, then we do not want to work against Him by interfering with His punishments through relieving the affliction of others.

However, when we believe that disaster, disease, and death fall randomly on good and bad alike, then we have no compunctions about indiscriminately abating the misery. Therefore we can respond to emergency situations without asking any questions. We can bring healing to the heart attack victim without investigating his lifestyle. As Christians we can offer health care to the cancer patient without researching her moral status. Grace enables us to offer shelter to hurricane victims without inquiring into their church affiliation, or provide rice and water to a starving mother without probing into her sins. Men and women who sense their unmerited forgiveness can dispense blankets to earthquake survivors without researching their past. All because a religion based on a theology of grace frees us to manifest indiscriminate kindness.

In short, like Jesus Christ, we can embody grace.

---

[1] For more of Job's thoughts see Job 6:30; 9:14-17; 12:4; 13:23; 16:16, 17; 21:7-18; 24:1; and 30:20, 21.

[2] Let it be clear. One's theology does not provide salvation. (God alone does.) After all, theology is simply another way of describing ideas or thoughts or notions. Such abstractions are powerless to save. However, concepts of God

(theological ideas) *effect* religion.

Once again, though, religion does not provide salvation. (God alone does.) But religion is pretty much theology in action—in other words, experience. And religion *affects* behavior.

So we can put it another way: theology does not save us but directly *effects* our religion and indirectly, therefore, *affects* us—our everyday experience.

[3] Linguists aren't certain of the precise meaning. Etymologically, it means either raw sewage or dog food.

[4] Aren't Jewish people today often generous and benevolent? My dad used to say that he enjoyed soliciting funds from Jews because they tend to be interested in relieving suffering. So is the distinction that ends this chapter invalid? I think not. Contemporary Jews do not espouse the first-century Judaism of the extreme Pharisees and also are not known for stressing ancient Deuteronomistic theology.

## WHEN GOD'S HEART BREAKS:

*"As a young man marries a maiden, so will your sons marry you; as a bridegroom rejoices over his bride, so will your God rejoice over you" (Isa. 62:5).*

# CHAPTER ELEVEN

## "This Will Hurt Me More Than It Will Hurt You"

Young—maybe 8 years old—and in big trouble, you could detect the seriousness of the circumstances because your dad (or was it your mother?) ordered, "Come here this very minute . . ." Your parent's voice sounded terribly stern. Additionally, he or she addressed you by your full name—first, middle, and last! You may not have had the IQ of Albert Einstein, but you knew that you were in for more than a lecture, even more than simply being sent to your room for a designated period of time.

Head hanging, you stiffly approached your parent. Inside you tried to steel yourself emotionally for the corporal punishment that you knew awaited you. Might the punishment come via belt or hand? As you stopped just in front of the seat of justice, your parent continued berating you, mincing no words in describing the gravity of your behavior and, furthermore, your audacity in perpetrating such a dastardly infraction of cherished family values. This assessment of your character made you wince. After pronouncing the form of physical discipline soon to be administered, you heard intoned firmly, "You know, don't you, that this will hurt *me* more than it will hurt *you*?"

And do you recall what you said in response? Oh, I don't mean out loud. No. But inside your mind you countered, "Yeah, sure!" (And after the confrontation ended, you don't recall your parent whimpering in pain, but you surely did!)

Remember how you detested it when your mother or dad

told you that the punishment about to be inflicted upon you was going to hurt him or her more than it would hurt you? You thought those words were the epitome of hypocrisy.

Then some 20 years later you found yourself irritated through and through with something that your own child had done. The gall your child had to behave like *that!* In stentorian tones you barked, "Come here right this very minute . . ." and you spat out your child's full name—first, middle, and last. When your offspring slunk over to where you stood, you explained in no uncertain terms that you were about to give him or her the thrashing of his or her life. And suddenly you heard yourself saying, "I want you to know that this is going to hurt *me* more than it will hurt *you!*"

Probably you could hardly believe your ears. In fact, your little sermon startled you. And if you hadn't been so peeved, you would have begun laughing as you heard those words tumble from your mouth. But you bit your lip and proceeded to administer what you felt was the appropriate corporal punishment for your child's misdemeanor.

In the chapter entitled "Sunshine and Rain" we talked about what theologians call Deuteronomistic theology. We demonstrated practically to the point of ad nauseam that the idea of moral cause and effect permeates the entire Old Testament. Almost in a single voice (with just a few exceptions), the biblical writers insisted that when God's people obeyed Him, good things would happen to them, but when they disobeyed Him, bad things would occur. "Keep My covenant and be blessed," we quoted God as saying, "or break My covenant and be cursed."

And the Old Testament writers were not afraid of talking about God's anger and portraying His fury. The language they used to describe His actions was strong, even explicitly offensive. Here's just a sampling of what you'll find in the prophets.

Isaiah raised his voice against God's people. "The Lord's *anger burns* against his people; *his hand is raised and he strikes them down.* . . . His anger is not turned away, his hand is still upraised" (Isa. 5:25). In chapter 9 Isaiah repeats himself: "His anger is not turned away, his hand is still upraised" (verse 12).

Verse 17 gets even more specific: "Therefore the Lord will take no pleasure in the young men, nor will he pity the fatherless and widows, for everyone is ungodly and wicked, every mouth speaks vileness. Yet for all this, his anger is not turned away, his hand is still upraised."[1] That refrain "his hand is still upraised" repeats itself several times in Isaiah and is graphic imagery.

Jeremiah offered colorful language as he quoted God: "Like a wind from the east, I will scatter them before their enemies; *I will show them my back* and not my face in the day of their disaster" (Jer. 18:17). Notice that God would turn away from His people just as human beings turn their back on someone.

God, through Ezekiel, referred to His "four dreadful judgments": sword, famine, wild animals, and plague (Eze. 14:21). Furthermore, God said: "The end is now upon you and I will unleash my anger against you. . . . I will not look on you with pity or spare you. . . . An unheard-of disaster is coming. . . . I will not look on you with pity or spare you; I will repay you in accordance with your conduct" (Eze. 7:3-9). Additionally, God said: "I the Lord have spoken. The time has come for me to act. I will not hold back; I will not have pity, nor will I relent" (Eze. 24:14). Ezekiel had God refusing to look on His people. He would respond to their behavior without pity.

Hosea quoted God as uttering even stronger words: "I will no longer show love to the house of Israel" (Hosea 1:6). Ouch! Modern instructors of parents tell them not to punish their children in anger. They urge parents always to discipline in love. Even more important, parents should never tell their children that they no longer will love them because of their bad behavior. Instead, parents should manifest unconditional love. But God said He'd behave differently. Then He got even more graphic: "I will strip her naked. . . . I will not show my love to her children" (Hosea 2:3, 4). Going naked meant the utmost in degradation and indignity for Israelites. But God wasn't through with His tirade: "For I will be like a lion to Ephraim, like a great lion to Judah. I will tear them to pieces and go away" (Hosea 5:14). God would behave as if He were a predatory jungle cat.[2]

Through Micah God made additional threats. "Therefore,

the Lord says: 'I am planning disaster against this people'" (Micah 2:3). Note that God was making definite plans—it was not a whim of the moment. Planning connotes a volitional, not an emotional, source. Intellectually and willfully God was considering the situation and inventing—yes, the word can connote that—something dire. "I will give you over to ruin and your people to derision" (Micah 6:16).

Zechariah reported: "The Lord Almighty was very angry. 'When I called, they did not listen; so when they called, I would not listen,' says the Lord Almighty" (Zech. 7:12, 13). And God also proclaimed: "My anger burns . . . , and I will punish" (Zech. 10:3).[3]

Zephaniah also quoted God as He vented His ire. "I will bring distress on the people and they will walk like blind men, because they have sinned against the Lord. Their blood will be poured out like dust and their entrails like filth" (Zeph. 1:17). In today's language, God threatened to spill their guts—and said so. The prophet spoke of "the day of the Lord's wrath." "He will make a sudden end of all who live in the earth" (verse 18). The Hebrew behind the English expression "sudden end" here is interesting.

The word translated "sudden" in Hebrew is *bahal*. It comes from a root meaning to quiver and so could refer to something that terrifies or perplexes. Here the verb has become a participle, which means that it is acting as an adjective to describe simple but continued action. So as an adjective it came to mean something alarming or rash or overhasty—reckless or impetuous. The word translated "end" is *kalah*, which expresses the extreme limit of something. It can be used positively, or negatively, as it is here in this context, in which it means an extreme or utter finality. Nothing will be left. One could translate it as "riddance." God, then, was promising reckless obliteration, rash extermination for His disobedient people. A devil-may-care Mr. Terminix would show up in the land, if you please.

"I have decided to assemble the nations, to gather the kingdoms and to pour out my wrath on them—all my fierce anger. The whole world will be consumed by the fire of my jealous anger" (Zeph. 3:8).

And Malachi, the last prophet of our Old Testament Bible, cited God's same refrain. "'If you do not listen, . . .' says the Lord Almighty, 'I will send a curse upon you. . . . I will spread on your faces the offal from your festival sacrifices'" (Mal. 2:2, 3). In case you missed the point, let me state it in plain English. God here promises to smear feces on their faces.

When I was in seventh and eighth grades, my parents sent me to Miss Regalbuto for accordion lessons. I was sitting in her parlor one afternoon to wait my turn when John's mother came to pick up her son, who had just finished having his instruction. Miss Regalbuto informed her that she needed pay for John's lesson.

Suddenly the boy's mother flew into a rage. It seems that she had given him the money for the lesson but that he had spent it on candy and soda. "I'm going to skin you alive," she screamed, and she proceeded to stomp around the room in a futile attempt to find something she could pick up and hit him with. Unfortunately (or fortunately, as the case may be), Miss Regalbuto had ornate lamps and vases and other decorative items in the parlor that would have shattered against John's unyielding body.

Finally, John's mother pulled out some money from her purse and paid Miss Regalbuto. As she yanked John out onto the porch and down the front stairs, she continued berating him and threatening to all but kill him when they got home.

The episode so unnerved Miss Regalbuto that her sister had to come in to give me my instruction, and I myself was quivering inside and didn't perform well that day. (OK, if the truth be known, I was never a star performer on any musical instrument.) When my dad came by to take me home, I pleaded with him to contact John's mother immediately, because I was certain that John's life was in jeopardy. But somehow Dad didn't take the mother's rantings as seriously as I did.

I wonder if God's people took His threatenings as seriously as they might have. Apparently not, for why did so many prophets have to come along and repeat God's dire warnings of judgment? But He did follow through on His threats (unlike John's mother). Israel suffered one disaster after another—plagues, famines, attacks from marauders.

However, this is only a partial picture. The prophets also portrayed a deeply passionate God who would back off in mercy—just as John's mother did, for (sure enough) John was back in school the next day and none the worse for wear. God not only called Israel and Judah His children and His people but also His wife and lover. As a result, He used strong emotional language to describe His relationship with His covenant people in both good times and bad. Just as graphic as His incensed words were so were His words of tender and poignant compassion.

Let's start with Isaiah again. "The Lord has spoken: 'I reared children and brought them up, but they have rebelled against me. The ox knows his master, the donkey his owner's manger, but Israel does not know, my people do not understand'" (Isa. 1:2, 3). Already we can hear God's heart breaking. He bemoaned the fact that dumb beasts of burden know their owners, but Israel, the very people whom He'd raised as His own children, did not know Him.

But there's more. Lots more. Because of their waywardness, God had to punish His recalcitrant children. Yet even then—in the very act of disciplining them—God's great heart hurt for them. It was as though He wanted to say, "This is hurting Me more than it is hurting you." Hear His words: "Why should you be beaten anymore? Why do you persist in rebellion? Your whole head is injured, your whole heart afflicted" (verse 5). God was clearly grieved that He'd had to resort to bruising His mulish people.

Isaiah recorded yet more tender expressions. "I will sing for the one I love a song" (Isa. 5:1). Yes, He is a singing God, a God who crooned love songs about and for His children. And in this same chapter He described Israel as a vineyard, but a vineyard that did not produce lusciously sweet fruit. Somehow God the Master Gardener, the One who had created the perfect Garden of Eden, had failed. What had happened to His green thumb, anyway? "What more could have been done for my vineyard than I have done for it?" (verse 4).

The prophet declared God's intentions. "The Lord will have

compassion on Jacob" (Isa. 14:1). The Hebrew word translated "compassion" is highly evocative. We can take a clue to its meaning by recounting the story of King Solomon and the feuding mothers.

Two women of questionable character lived in the same house, and each gave birth to baby boys a mere three days apart. One night Mama B's son died, so she tiptoed into Mama A's room and switched infants, giving Mama A the corpse.

When Mama A awakened that morning and prepared to nurse her child, she made two disconcerting discoveries: (1) the baby was dead and (2) it was not her infant lying by her side but Mama B's child.

Before long the two squabbling women appeared before Judge Solomon for a ruling. Solomon listened to their sworn testimony, and it didn't take a Solomon to deduce that one of the mothers was lying, but it did take Solomonic wisdom to figure out which one was the real mother.

At the end of their testimony, the king called for a soldier and ordered him to slice the living baby in two and give a half to each woman.

Mama B replied, "Good idea!"

But Mama A said, "OK, give the baby to her."

Solomon thereupon decided that the surviving infant belonged to Mama A, who "was filled with compassion" for the baby (1 Kings 3:26) and was willing to give him up as long as it would spare his life.

There's that word again—compassion. The Hebrew literally says that her *rahamim* "grew warm." Just what part of this woman's body grew warm? "Difficult to translate in the fullness of its imagery, the Hebrew noun *rahamim* connotes simultaneously birth as a mode of being and the locus of that mode. In its singular form the noun *rehem* means 'womb' or 'uterus.' In the plural, *rahamim,* this concrete meaning expands to the abstractions of compassion, mercy, and love. Further, these abstractions occur in a verb, *rhm,* 'to show mercy,' and in an adjective, *rahum,* 'merciful'" (Phyllis Trible, *God and the Rhetoric of Sexuality,* p. 33).

In short, the word "womb" in Hebrew is a metaphor—a figure of speech. Now, linguists when they talk about metaphors
speak of the *vehicle* of the metaphor and its *tenor*. The vehicle
corresponds to the literal meaning of the metaphor. For example, when Jesus said "I am the door" He was using a metaphor.
The wooden object that swung on hinges was the *vehicle* of that
imagery. The concept that Jesus provided access to God, for instance, was the *tenor*.

So with the Hebrew root *rhm*. The *vehicle* was the anatomi-
cal body part known today as the uterus. The *tenor* was a state
of mind or "psychic mode of being" *(ibid.)*. "Although the vehicle womb is an organ unique to women, men also participate
in the journey of this biblical metaphor" *(ibid.)*. And often in
Scripture it is a "journey from the wombs of women to the compassion of God" *(ibid., p. 34)*.

In essence Isaiah insisted that God would be "wombish," an
interesting way of expressing the Hebrew that Marcus Borg suggests in his book *Meeting Jesus Again for the First Time* (p. 48).
"Like a womb, God is the one who gives birth to us. . . . God
loves us and feels for us. . . . *Compassionate* has nuances of giving life, nourishing, caring, perhaps embracing and encompassing" *(ibid.)*.

The Hebrew can also refer to fondling and soothing someone. God "will be a father to those who live in Jerusalem and to
the house of Judah" (Isa. 22:21). "The Sovereign Lord will wipe
away the tears from all faces" (Isa. 25:8). In this imagery God
would whip out His hanky and tenderly blot the tears from His
people's faces—a lovely picture, indeed. He would put bandages
on the wounds of His people and heal them (Isa. 30:26).

"The Lord longs to be gracious to you; he rises to show you
compassion. . . . How gracious he will be when you cry for help!
As soon as he hears, he will answer you" (verses 18, 19). In the
King James Version this verse begins "Therefore will the Lord
wait." But there is another way of rendering the Hebrew verb
here, which the translators of the NIV chose and which is probably more accurate given the context: God awaits the time when
He can be gracious; He craves being gracious, which in the

Hebrew has the idea of bending or stooping in mercy to do something kind, as when an adult squats down to give a small child a lollipop.

And so God instructed Isaiah what he should say. *"Comfort, comfort my people,* says your God. Speak tenderly to Jerusalem" (Isa. 40:1, 2). The Hebrew word here is *nacham,* and the root idea is to breathe heavily or to sigh. It came to mean be sorry for or to comfort, because such heavy breathing was a physical expression of one's emotions.

Isaiah next used a different metaphor, that of a shepherd. "See, the Sovereign Lord comes . . . He tends his flock like a shepherd: He gathers the lambs in his arms and carries them close to his heart; he gently leads those that have young" (verses 10, 11).

In reassuring tones God said: "So do not fear, for I am with you; do not be dismayed, for I am your God. I will strengthen you and help you" (Isa. 41:10). "I am the Lord, your God, who takes hold of your right hand and says to you, Do not fear; I will help you" (verse 13).

Next God likened Himself to a pregnant woman ready to give birth. "For a long time I have kept silent. . . . But now, like a woman in childbirth, I cry out, I gasp and pant" (Isa. 42:14). Wow, all this really was hurting God as much as or more than it hurt His people! God said here (in our English translation) that He had kept silent "for a long time." The Hebrew says that He had remained quiet for eternity—forever! But no longer.

And notice this: "Even to your old age and gray hairs I am he, I am he who will sustain you. I have made you and I will carry you" (Isa. 46:4). It didn't matter that they had gray hair, that they were old and up in years. God would continue to carry them. Now that my two sons are adults, I enjoy going on hikes with them. No longer do I hear them whining, "Please carry me, Daddy. I'm tired. I can't walk. Please pick me up. Carry me!" So it's fun now to go on long walks with them. I feel relieved that I no longer have to carry them in my arms or on my back. But not so with God. No matter how old His people were, He still promised to pick them up and carry them!

"The Lord comforts his people and will have compassion on

his afflicted ones. But Zion said, 'The Lord has forsaken me, the Lord has forgotten me.' 'Can a mother forget the baby at her breast and have no compassion on the child she has borne? Though she may forget, I will not forget you! See, I have engraved you on the palms of my hands'" (Isa. 49:13-16). God was even more caring than a mother breastfeeding her infant because His love never fails and cannot be shaken (Isa. 54:10).

The prophet switched to yet another figure of speech. "For your Maker is your husband—the Lord Almighty is his name. . . . 'For a brief moment I abandoned you, but with deep compassion I will bring you back. In a surge of anger I hid my face from you for a moment, but with everlasting kindness I will have compassion on you'" (verses 5-8). "As a bridegroom rejoices over his bride, so will your God rejoice over you" (Isa. 62:5). Can't you just envision God as a beaming groom? I've been to many weddings, and I don't recall ever seeing a gloomy, morose groom. Usually they are all smiles and solicitous. A groom has an eagerness on his face matched only by the glow on the bride's countenance.

"I will create Jerusalem to be a delight and its people a joy. I will rejoice over Jerusalem and take delight in my people; the sound of weeping and of crying will be heard in it no more" (Isa. 65:18, 19). "To a nation that did not call on my name, I said, 'Here am I, here am I.' All day long I have held out my hands to an obstinate people" (verses 1, 2). God poignantly explained here that He called again and again "Here I am" as He held out His hands to Israel.[4]

Let's move on to Jeremiah, through whom God pleaded with His people for some kind of explanation for their wayward behavior. You can hear the pathos in His voice. "This is what the Lord says: 'What fault did your fathers find in me, that they strayed so far from me?'"(Jer. 2:5).

A young woman would hardly lose track of her expensive jewelry, yet the infinite God is apparently incapable of counting the number of days that His people had forgotten Him. "Does a maiden forget her jewelry, a bride her wedding ornaments? Yet my people have forgotten me, days without number" (verse 32).

You'd almost think that Jeremiah were Hosea because of the terms of endearment that he related God as using. "'Return, faithless Israel,' declares the Lord, 'I will frown on you no longer, for I am merciful. . . . I am your husband'" (Jer. 3:12-14). "I myself said, 'How gladly would I treat you like sons and give you a desirable land. . . . I thought you would call me "Father" and not turn away from following me. But like a woman unfaithful to her husband, so you have been unfaithful to me, O house of Israel'" (verses 19, 20). God had hoped that the Israelites would call Him "Father," but He said that His hopes were in vain.

But regardless of how His people treated Him, He would deal with them as He always intended. "'For I know the plans I have for you,' declares the Lord, 'plans to prosper you and not to harm you, plans to give you hope and a future'" (Jer. 29:11). Oh, how God's great heart aches!

"'Is not Ephraim my dear son, the child in whom I delight? Though I often speak against him, I still remember him. Therefore my heart yearns for him; I have great compassion for him,' declares the Lord" (Jer. 31:20). I can almost hear God's sobs, can't you, as He bemoans the way His people have treated Him.

You may have noticed Jeremiah's use of the word "compassion" again. The word employed in Jeremiah 31:20 is very graphic. First, YHWH said, "Though I often speak against him, I still remember him." That is one possible way to translate the Hebrew, but not the only way.

The various versions render this part of the verse in differing ways—some more negatively or more harshly than others. The context, however, seems to rule out harshness. So the English wording can be "For the more I speak of him, the more I do remember him" (Phyllis Trible, *God and the Rhetoric of Sexuality*, p. 45). When God mentioned the name of His child Ephraim, fond memories flooded His mind, and the more He uttered "Ephraim," the more His infinite heart overflowed with yearning.

But there's more. God continued: "Therefore my heart yearns for him; I have great compassion for him." Here God used language that appears to come directly from the Song of

Solomon, where Solomon's lover described her erotic passion this way: "My lover thrust his hand through the latch-opening; *my heart began to pound for him*" (Song of Sol. 5:4). Admittedly, the English renditions don't sound very erotic when they translate this verse, but then the Bible is supposed to be a family book, is it not? Nevertheless, the imagery in Song of Solomon gives it what we would call an adult rating![5]

On this reading, since God in Jeremiah 31:20 used the same Hebrew as in Song of Solomon, the verse could be properly translated "Therefore . . . I become wombish [to use the term coined by biblical scholar Marcus Borg] for" Ephraim.

But punishment would come if they did not mend their ways. So God tried to reason with them. Perhaps He could talk them out of the perverseness. "Now this is what the Lord God Almighty, the God of Israel, says: Why bring such great disaster on yourselves?" (Jer. 44:7).

And even if God must impose ever so severe punishment, He remained unchanged in His passionate adoration. "Though he brings grief, he will show compassion, so great is his unfailing love. For he does not willingly bring affliction or grief to the children of men" (Lam. 3:32, 33). When Jeremiah wrote that God "does not willingly bring affliction," he literally said that it does not come from God's heart. In other words, the punishment He administers isn't heartfelt.

The Old Testament refers to the heart many hundreds of times (814 times for the human heart; 26 times for God's "heart"; and 11 times the "heart of the sea"). Most of the time the word appears it is not so much a literal reference anatomically as it is a metaphorical statement. As a Hebrew metaphor the heart had a wider range of connotations than the same English metaphor.

For us the word "heart" says Valentine's Day, when we give heart-shaped boxes of chocolates and heart-embellished cards to those we love. In the Old Testament the body part that would have been used on Valentine's Day (if they had one) would more likely have been the "reins," or kidneys. (Can't you just see yourself giving your sweetheart a kidney-shaped box of chocolates or a card bedecked with a kidney with an arrow piercing it?)

To the ancient Hebrew mind "the heart [was] the center of emotions, feelings, moods, and passions" *(Harper's Bible Dictionary,* p. 377). It also "function[ed] as the source of thought and reflection" *(ibid.).* And in addition to this intellectual aspect of the heart, it also represented "the idea of volition" *(ibid.).*

So when God says that His reproof doesn't come from His heart, He means that it doesn't reflect His inherent nature. God really doesn't have the heart to do this, but He must even though His heart isn't in it. Something foreign to Him, it does not correspond with His emotions, feelings, moods, passions, mind, or will. That's why some of the versions render it that God does not do this willingly, though even that seems to narrow the nuanced meaning of the Hebrew.[6]

Ezekiel also portrayed God's strong emotional attachment to His people. "I have been grieved by their adulterous hearts" (Eze. 6:9). The New Revised Standard Version translates this as "I was crushed." The Hebrew verb here means to shatter, to burst, to smash. Thirty-three times in the Old Testament the Bible writers applied this verb to God Himself *(The Complete Word Study of the Old Testament,* p. 2370).

"Turn away from all your offenses; then sin will not be your downfall. . . . Why will you die, O house of Israel? For I take no pleasure in the death of anyone, declares the Sovereign Lord. Repent and live!" (Eze. 18:30-32). God's voice has a catch in it, don't you think, when He says this. "Turn! Turn from your evil ways! Why will you die, O house of Israel?" (Eze. 33:11).[7]

Through Hosea God continued to express His pathos. You'll recall that much of the book of Hosea relates the prophet's experience with his philandering wife, Gomer. This deeply personal and distressing experience for Hosea became a living metaphor of God's relationship with His people Israel.

To use the technical metaphorical terminology again: Gomer's philandering was the *vehicle,* and Israel's idolatrous disobedience was the *tenor.* Also Hosea's heartbreak was the *vehicle,* and God's stunning grief was the *tenor.*

"What can I do with you, Ephraim? What can I do with you,

Judah? Your love is like the morning mist, like the early dew that disappears" (Hosea 6:4). An interesting simile here, isn't it? Not only is Israel's love for God as insubstantial as mist or fog, but it is also as quick to evaporate.

"When Israel was a child, I loved him" (Hosea 11:1). The Hebrew verb here is *ahab* (pronounced *ahav*). It connotes a wide range of feelings just as does the English verb "love." Not only does the word embrace fondness, but it also indicates close attachment. "It implies an ardent and vehement inclination of the mind and a tenderness of affection at the same time" *(ibid.,* p. 2298). It's the same word used in Genesis 37:3 to describe Jacob's doting fondness for his son Joseph.

And God was a coddling and patient parent. "It was I who taught Ephraim to walk, taking them by the arms. . . . I led them with cords of human kindness, with ties of love; I lifted the yoke from their neck and bent down to feed them" (Hosea 11:3, 4). God helped His child take his first faltering step, holding Ephraim's arms while he tottered on his tiptoes. And in great condescension God bent down to feed His little one.

Little wonder, then, that God's heart broke when He thought of having to let go of His errant child. "How can I give you up, Ephraim? How can I hand you over, Israel? . . . My heart is changed within me; all my compassion is aroused" (verse 8). When God declares that His heart is changed, He is saying that it is overthrown, turned over, destroyed because circumstances have kindled His compassion or desire to comfort.

So God made up His mind. He would go out of His way to be faithful even if His children weren't faithful to Him. "I will heal their waywardness and love them freely, for my anger has turned away from them. I will be like the dew to Israel" (Hos. 14:4, 5). Dew is a major source of moisture for vegetation in Palestine, especially during the dry season.

Joel also described a forgiving God. "Rend your heart and not your garments. Return to the Lord your God, for he is gracious and compassionate, slow to anger and abounding in love, and he relents from sending calamity" (Joel 2:13). The Hebrew adjective *channun* translated "gracious" is used only of God.

"Then the Lord will be jealous for his land and take pity on his people" (verse 18). The concept behind the Hebrew word for jealous *(qana)* means to turn red. When someone turns beet red, he or she is experiencing a strong emotion, generally of either jealousy or anger (the two often go together, don't they?).

Amos too had something to say about God's passion for His people. The prophet had just seen the terrible plight they would soon be in, and he was appalled. "When they had stripped the land clean, I cried out, 'Sovereign Lord, forgive! How can Jacob survive? He is so small!' So the Lord relented. 'This will not happen,' the Lord said" (Amos 7:2, 3). When Amos reminded YHWH that His people were tiny, God mercifully relented. "'I will not totally destroy the house of Jacob,' declares the Lord" (Amos 9:8).

Through Micah God again became introspective and wondered what He might have done wrong in dealing with Israel. "My people, what have I done to you? How have I burdened you? Answer me" (Micah 6:3). Maybe He hadn't been the perfect parent that He thought He was. Did Israel have any insights for Him as to what He could do better? No. God sounded like a concerned parent confronting a delinquent child.

"Who is a God like you, who pardons sin and forgives the transgression of the remnant of his inheritance? You do not stay angry forever but delight to show mercy" (Micah 7:18).

Zechariah had a glorious prophecy. "The Lord Almighty will care for his flock, the house of Judah, and make them like a proud horse in battle" (Zech. 10:3). "I will keep a watchful eye over the house of Judah" (Zech. 12:4). Again we detect a sense of tenderness as God promised to keep an open eye over His people.

It seems that God's prophets hammered the point home. Even in times when He must punish His intractable people, His heart ached for them. His compassion overflowed. He simply didn't have His heart in the severe but corrective measures that He felt were required.

And although God didn't use exactly the same words your parents used on you and me, the idea is still there. All this was indeed hurting Him as much or even more than it was hurting

His people. That's why Isaiah could declare: "In all their afflic-tion he was afflicted" (Isa. 63:9, KJV). The word translated "af-fliction" meant narrows or a tight spot and so came to extend to rough times, hard times, tribulation, disaster. The troubles and distress that overwhelmed His people caused Him also trouble and distress. In short, God hurt when they hurt.

In Judges 10:16 we read that God's "soul was grieved for the misery of Israel" (KJV). First of all we need to note what God saw: Israel's "misery." The word is *amal* and describes hard labor, distress, trouble, sorrow, suffering. The Hebrew noun here described what Israel was enduring under the oppression of the Philistines and Ammonites. And when they first cried to God, He seemed indifferent and said: "Go and cry unto the gods which ye have chosen; let them deliver you in the time of your tribulation" (verse 14, KJV).

But the more God saw of their pain, the more His heart broke. Finally, the passage says that His "soul was grieved." The word translated "soul" is *nephesh* and means life. The Hebrew word rendered "grieved" means to dock—as you dock a dog's tail; you cut it off. It also means to harvest or to curtail. So what the imagery here indicated was that when God saw the troubles and afflictions of His people, it docked, curtailed, cut short His own life.

I suppose that we can't take the words literally, because God is immortal and self-sustaining. He can't die. And so it is that translators have a hard time with this verse. The New Revised Standard Version translates it this way: "He could no longer bear to see Israel suffer." The New International Version says: "He could bear Israel's misery no longer." *The Anchor Bible* ren-ders it: "The plight of Israel became intolerable to him." *The Jerusalem Bible* phrases: "He could bear Israel's suffering no longer." Nevertheless, the metaphor here is about as strong im-agery as one could get. Even the life of the eternal God became shortened or was being reaped or lopped off!

❤ ❤ ❤

Of course, all the references we have surveyed were talking

about how God felt when He had to punish Israel and Judah. At those times when, according to Deuteronomistic theology, God jumped into history and purposely saw to it that His rebellious people were hurt severely, He Himself suffered along with them. And if God was so passionate when He was in the very act of reprimanding His guilty people, it is only logical that He must be even far more compassionate when He sees His innocent people suffer.

We need not simply jump to that conclusion. When we look in the New Testament and study the life of Jesus, the One who focused God most sharply for us, we find our conclusion explicitly presented.

First, we note that not even a tiny sparrow dies without God noticing it (Matt. 10:29; cf. Luke 12:6). Now, I'm a bird watcher of sorts, but I hardly pay much attention to sparrows. When I'm driving along, I crane my neck to see the vultures and the red-shouldered hawks and the kestrels—but not for sparrows. Yet God watches them. He remembers them and is aware when one dies!

Second, God takes such an interest in you—and me—that Jesus described His care as keeping a running count of the hairs on our head (Matt. 10:30; Luke 12:7). Perhaps you take that statement literally. I believe that the God of the universe, despite His infinity, has more to do than keep a running tally on how many hairs every one of the billions of earth's inhabitants has. Nonetheless, I regard it as a particularly telling metaphor. God is interested in you—and me—more than we can even imagine. He is concerned about everything that affects us—even the minutia of life.

Third, the Gospels constantly describe Jesus as being moved with compassion. When He saw the crowds flocking to Him, He had compassion on them (Matt. 9:36). Climbing out of the boat and seeing so many sick people, "he had compassion on them and healed their sick" (Matt. 14:14). As 4,000 eager people got hungry while listening to Jesus teach, He had compassion on them (Matt. 15:32). Leaving Jericho and encountering two blind men, He had compassion on them and restored their sight (Matt. 20:34). Jesus was filled with compassion when He met a man with leprosy (Mark 1:41). When Jesus visited the town of Nain and saw the widow weeping because her only son was being carried to the grave, He had compassion on her and raised the boy to life (Luke 7:13-15).

Fourth, when Jesus finally made it to Bethany and stood by Lazarus's grave, He was moved to tears (John 11:35). (You'll recall that this poignant passage has the fame of being the shortest verse in the English Bible.)

Fifth, during His triumphal entry when, from the Mount of Olives, Jesus looked down on Jerusalem and contemplated her destruction, His great heart seemed to be on the verge of breaking. "As he approached Jerusalem and saw the city, he wept over it" (Luke 19:41). And later in the Temple Jesus bemoaned Jerusalem's fate: "O Jerusalem, Jerusalem, . . . how often I have longed to gather your children together, as a hen gathers her chicks under her wings, but you were not willing" (Matt. 23:37).

Sixth, Peter instructs us to cast all our cares upon Him, "because he cares for [us]" (1 Peter 5:7).

Clearly, then, whatever suffering may come our way, we can rest assured that our heavenly Father knows what we're experiencing, because He's going through it with us. He cares for us with an interest more intense than any we could possibly ever imagine. When our hearts break, His is breaking also because in all our sufferings He suffers too. This is what you—and I—should tell those quavering under the onslaught of disaster, disease, and death.

Sometimes when we read in the newspapers about or see on TV the individual cases of disaster, disease, and death that the media report, we shudder and finally feel that we must block it all out before we go crazy. If such suffering raises this kind of pity and emotion in us, just imagine how God must feel, because He knows about not only these specific cases but also all those incidences of suffering scourging our planet that never make the news. He sees it all, and it must take an infinite God to be able to hold up under the strain of all that comes to His attention.

In Zechariah 2:8 we read: "Whoever touches you touches the apple of [God's] eye." Other texts use the same expression of God's people (Deut. 32:10 and Ps. 17:8). The point is that if anyone attacked God's people, it would be like hitting Him in the eyeball. To touch God's people was like poking a finger in His eye.

So although we may have been cynical about our parents' words that when they punished us they were going to hurt more than we, we can rest assured that such is indeed the case with our loving, compassionate God. When we suffer, He suffers too.

---

[1] Here is a list of references that support the same theme: Isa. 5:25; 9:11, 12, 17, 19, 21; 10:25; 12:1; 24:5, 6; 26:20, 21; and 29:5, 6.

[2] Here are more verses that speak of God's anger: Hosea 1:6; 2:3, 4, 11; 5:14; 9:15; and 13:7.

[3] Here are verse references in Zechariah that speak of God's anger: 7:12-14 and 10:3.

[4] Here is a list of verses in Isaiah that speak of God's impassioned yearning: 1:2, 3, 5; 5:1, 4; 12:1; 14:1; 22:21; 25:6, 8; 30:18-21, 26; 40:1, 2, 10, 11; 41:8-10, 13; 42:14; 46:4; 49:13-16; 52:10; 54:5-8, 10; 55:7; 62:5; 65:2; and 65:18, 19.

[5] Five Hebrew words here in Song of Solomon get very explicit. The verbs and nouns as translated into English sound quite innocent. However, in ancient Hebrew culture the verbs and nouns were loaded with meaning—sexual meaning.

For example, in English a crass man might refer to a woman as "stacked." The verb has a perfectly legitimate use when describing the action of piling one thing upon another. But in slang usage the term refers to the female figure.

This is not the place to go into the explicit details, but the language of Song of Solomon is erotic.

[6] Here is a list of verses in Jeremiah that speak of God's impassioned yearning: 2:2, 5, 32; 3:12-15, 19, 20; 5:7; 29:11, 13, 14; 31:20; and 44:7.

[7] Here is a list of verses in Ezekiel that speak of God's impassioned yearning: 6:9; 18:30-32; and 33:11.

## WHEN GOD'S HEART BREAKS:

*"I said, 'Here am I, here am I.' All day long I have held out my hands to an obstinate people, who walk in ways not good, pursuing their own imaginations" (Isa. 65:2).*

# CHAPTER TWELVE

## Louie, Part Two

You'll recall that chapter 1 relates the moving story of my friend Louie. That chapter ended with Louie's life cut short at the early age of 49. However, I really want to say more about this tragic episode, and so I end this book with further reflections on Louie and Heidi's experience.

My friend Gerald and I were talking about Louie and Heidi's plight—the physical pain, the emotional pain, the spiritual pain. I bitterly referred to those audacious friends who had consoled Louie and Heidi with their nasty comments.

But Gerald defended them—well, at least he explained their reactions. "Michelle's death was so threatening to them because they were terrified that the same thing just might happen to their own kids. So they had to come up with some kind of explanation that would provide a rationale for why such a terrible thing would *never* happen to their own children.

"It was their way of coping," he concluded.

Huh! Some way of coping! Sure, devastate someone else who is already hurting so that your own mind can rest at ease! Come on!

Of course, intellectually I have to admit that Gerald had a point, but emotionally I just cannot reconcile myself to such macabre behavior.

People like that don't deserve the name Christian! Do I even want to belong to the same denomination as they? After all, if what they did and said is the fruit of the teachings of a church, who wants any part of it?

And what about you? and me? What do we say to people in the throes of great misery and loss? What kind of excuses and pretexts do we give? What kind of rationales do we jabber to a grieving mother? What words of defense do we babble to an anguished father?

Do our weak-kneed, tepid defenses of God in the face of disaster, disease, and death simply pile further hurt upon already emotionally injured men and women, boys and girls? Do our flimsy and ineffectual theodicies merely heap additional damage upon already physically smarting people?

And what theological implications lurk behind our mutterings—well-meaning as they may be—when we impulsively parrot lame assurances and unpersuasive arguments?

Maybe we need to give a second thought—or more—before we open our mouths when we confront suffering. Maybe we need to take a cue from the first behavior of Job's friends. You remember biblical Job, don't you? And his friends? When they heard of his misfortunes, they came to visit him. At first they didn't even recognize their friend, and broke into weeping (Job 2:12). Then "they sat with him on the ground seven days and seven nights, and no one spoke a word to him" (verse 13, NRSV).

Louie and Heidi's friends should have imitated what Job's friends did initially, and not what they did later! And it's not bad behavior for you and me to emulate also!

But back to Gerald's explanation. As I sat in my office mentally grousing about his comments, a Bible verse flashed into my mind. It was Hebrews 2:11. Here's what it says: "For both he that sanctifieth and they who are sanctified are all of one: *for which cause he is not ashamed to call them brethren*" (KJV).

Ouch! Did you notice that last part of the verse? I've italicized it so that you wouldn't miss it. But notice it once again: "He is not ashamed to call them brethren."

First, maybe we need to find out just who this "he" is whom Scripture mentions. That would be helpful as we try to decipher the meaning of the passage. Earlier the chapter mentions angels, the Lord, the Holy Ghost, and Jesus. So the "he" might refer to any of them.

However, from verse 12 to the end of the chapter, it becomes increasingly clear that the individual in mind is Jesus Christ Himself. This Person is going to speak to His brethren and will sing their praises in the midst of the church (verse 12). The passage mentions God's children and then contrasts them with this Person who also was flesh and blood and who by death destroyed the devil (verse 14). This same individual, who took upon Himself the nature of Abraham, would then deliver those in bondage (verse 15). Indeed, in all things He was made like His brothers, and because of this He became a merciful and faithful high priest (verse 17). Since He Himself suffered temptation, He is able to succor or sustain the rest of us who also face constant temptation (verse 18).

It would be difficult to conclude anything else other than that the word "he" in Hebrews 2:11 refers to Jesus Himself.

But to whom does the word "them" in the verse refer? That's the next thing we must ascertain, isn't it?

Well, verse 6 quotes Psalm 8:4, which refers to "man" and the "son of man." "Son of man" here is simply a Hebrew idiom that often means "human being"—it's a generic term. And verse 9 tells us that "by the grace of God" He—Jesus—"should taste death for *every man*." The Greek word here is *pantos,* an adjective that means "all" or "everyone."

So can we infer from the context of this verse that Jesus isn't ashamed to call the human race His family—His brothers and sisters? Quite possibly.

But the verse itself seems to narrow the context a bit. It talks about those "who are sanctified." The Greek word here is a present passive middle participle. This means that something is being done to someone (passive) and that this action is continuous or repeated (present) contemporaneously (participle) with the main verb. The literal meaning, then, refers to those people who are in the process of being sanctified.

We'll stay with the more limited group. Jesus wasn't ashamed to call *them*—all who have accepted God and later Jesus as their Saviour—His relatives.

Let's see. Just whom might that include?

Well, there's God's "friend" Abraham—a good man but one prone to lying.

And Moses, a murderer and fugitive from justice.

And don't forget the judges: Samson, who behaved like an ancient James Bond—always in the wrong bed with the wrong woman, thereby jeopardizing his life, and always having to find a clever way to defeat the enemy. Gideon, who ended up with a name incorporating the term Baal, a heathen deity—Jerubbaal—and who became a self-worshiper after getting an inflated opinion of himself and the ephod he made!

Yes, consider David, a man after God's own heart, who slaughtered people right and left, who fell into adultery and then murder.

Don't overlook King Manasseh, one of the worst kings of Old Testament times even if he did repent toward the very end of his life.

Turning to the New Testament, we come upon Peter, who was so mercurial that Jesus could never count on him and who denied he ever knew Jesus—at the very moment Jesus was being tortured physically, emotionally, and spiritually.

And there was Saul, aka Paul, who did his utmost to exterminate Christianity.

Notice that I didn't mention any women. No problem.

Look at Eve, who first ate the forbidden fruit.

Don't forget about Tamar, Jacob's daughter-in-law, who disguised herself as a prostitute and got pregnant by her father-in-law, yet whom he described as more righteous than he!

And there was Rahab, the madam who sheltered the Israelite spies. (Whatever were they at the brothel for in the first place!)

Esther was that good Jewish girl who spent the night with a pagan king who had divorced his previous wife because she wouldn't flaunt her charms for his government cronies. And Esther pleased the king that night—more than all the other pagan girls in the beauty contest.

Mary Magdalene didn't need a Lamborghini in order to merit the description "fast."

But Jesus wasn't ashamed to call these—and countless

other—undesirables His brothers and sisters.

You get the idea, don't you?

Yes, Jesus was not embarrassed to call these defective men and women His relatives. His brothers. His sisters. He wanted to be the Saviour of each one back then and of each one ever since—including you and me!

That's right.

Jesus isn't ashamed to call you and me His brother, His sister—despite the things we've done that have brought embarrassment and grief to Him.

So I guess that I—with all my foibles, shortcomings, deficiencies, failings, defects, sins, vices, transgressions, depravity, corruption, baseness, vileness—should be more accepting of those ill-mannered so-called Christians who turned out to be "Job's comforters" to Louie and Heidi.

*Jesus* isn't ashamed to call them His relatives. And if Jesus, of all persons, is not ashamed to call them His brothers and His sisters, then surely I shouldn't find it so humiliating, so mortifying, so difficult, so onerous, to refer to them as "brother" and "sister."

Of course, Jesus' generosity doesn't minimize their rudeness to Louie and Heidi. It doesn't downplay their coarseness or diminish their nastiness. Nor does it ignore their indecency. Nonetheless, He isn't ashamed to call them "brethren," because He died for *them*. Precisely because they needed it and continue to need it. And the truth is that He died for *me* as well. Precisely because I needed it and continue to need it.

Yes, those Tennesseans should have shed tears with Louie and Heidi and comforted them in their terrible distress. They should have reassured Louie and Heidi of God's love, not of His judgment against some petty infractions. Each of them should have been more sensitive, sympathetic, compassionate, responsive, empathetic, benevolent, and merciful. No question about it.

Nevertheless, Jesus loves them so much that He isn't ashamed to call them "brethren" and to die for them and to work to make them holy.

His death shows that He doesn't ignore sin and evil and terror. It reveals that He wants to lift them—and you and me—out of our pettiness, our intolerance, our bigotry, our fanaticism, our narrowness—all our shortcomings, be they big or be they little.

God must have shed tears when those friends phoned Louie and Heidi with their unkind comments.

God must shed tears when you and I do things that expose our callousness and heartlessness.

God wants to remove our stony hearts and give us soft and tender and compassionate hearts.

Can I weep with Him?

And with Louie and Heidi?

And with others?

**Oh Jesus, You who wept with and for Mary and Martha and Jerusalem, please let my heart be broken with the things that break the heart of God.**

### WHEN GOD'S HEART BREAKS:
*"I will rejoice over Jerusalem and take delight in my people; the sound of weeping and of crying will be heard in it no more" (Isa. 65:19).*

"Does Jesus care when my heart is pained
    Too deeply for mirth or song;
    As the burdens press, and the cares distress,
    And the way grows weary and long?

        "O yes, He cares—
        I know He cares!
        His heart is touched with my grief;
        When the days are weary, the long nights dreary,
        I know my Saviour cares.

"Does Jesus care when my way is dark
    With a nameless dread and fear?
    As the daylight fades into deep night shades,
    Does He care enough to be near?

        "O yes, He cares—
        I know He cares!
        His heart is touched with my grief;
        When the days are weary, the long nights dreary,
        I know my Saviour cares.

"Does Jesus care when I've said goodbye
    To the dearest on earth to me,
    And my sad heart aches till it nearly breaks—
    Is it aught to Him? does He see?

        "O yes, He cares—
        I know He cares!
        His heart is touched with my grief;
        When the days are weary, the long nights dreary,
        I know my Saviour cares."
                                —Frank E. Graeff


"God permits evil in order to transform it into greater good"
(cited in *Reader's Digest*, July 1995, p. 198).

Also by Richard W. Coffen
# When God Sheds Tears

In this companion book to *When God's Heart Breaks,*
Richard Coffen explores other common explanations for suffering and demonstrates how they are inconsistent with what
God has revealed about Himself in Scripture. He shows how
accepting them can distort our concept of God, making it both
difficult to empathize with others and to love and trust Him
ourselves. He encourages us to relinquish harmful half-truths
and hold firm to the God of the Bible—a God who sheds
tears when we hurt and who has promised to abolish sin and
restore our joy.

Paper, 127 pages.
US$8.99, Cdn$12.99.